MISSION:MAN

LIFE LESSONS
FROM A
CIA OPERATIVE

MISSION:MAN

LIFE LESSONS
FROM A
CIA OPERATIVE

B.D. FOLEY

PLAIN SIGHT
PUBLISHING
An Imprint of Cedar Fort, Inc.
Springville, Utah

ISBN 13: 978-1-4621-1920-2

Published by Plain Sight Publishing, an imprint of Cedar Fort, Inc.
2373 W. 700 S., Springville, UT 84663
Distributed by Cedar Fort, Inc., www.cedarfort.com

LIBRARY OF CONGRESS CATALOGING-IN-PUBLICATION DATA

Names: Foley, B. D. (Brent Durwood), 1958- author.
Title: Mission man : life lessons from a CIA operative / B.D. Foley.
Description: Springville, Utah : Plain Sight Publishing, An imprint of Cedar
  Fort, Inc., [2016] | Includes bibliographical references and index.
Identifiers: LCCN 2016030603 (print) | LCCN 2016033185 (ebook) | ISBN
  9781462119202 (perfect bound : alk. paper) | ISBN 9781462127016 (epub,
  pdf, mobi)
Subjects: LCSH: Foley, B. D. (Brent Durwood), 1958- | Intelligence
  officers--Biography. | LCGFT: Autobiographies. | Humor. | Anecdotes.
Classification: LCC JK468.I6 F65 2016 (print) | LCC JK468.I6 (ebook) | DDC
  327.12730092 [B] --dc23
LC record available at https://lccn.loc.gov/2016030603

Cover design by Kinsey Beckett
Cover design © 2016 by Cedar Fort, Inc.
Edited and typeset by Jennifer Johnson

Printed in the United States of America

10 9 8 7 6 5 4 3 2 1

Printed on acid-free paper

To my two sons, Nolan and Brandon.

Also by B. D. Foley

CIA Street Smarts for Women

CONTENTS

Contents

FOREWORD

I remember a trip to Afghanistan, one of several missions to war zones. As other passengers and I disembarked late at night, we lined up outside our aircraft, facing the hangar, and waited alongside several cargo containers. Another group of men and women lined up across from us, facing the plane, all of them embarking passengers who were waiting for us to get off and out of the way so they could board. The two sides looked at each other in the dark, not talking, searching for familiar faces, but also exchanging thoughts, I'm sure. Those that were going home were undoubtedly thinking, *What a poor bunch.* And I'm sure that many of us who were arriving were thinking, *What a lucky bunch . . . Wouldn't it be nice to just switch lines and get back on the plane?*

I know that it might be tempting to switch lines in life. But if I had, I would have missed out on rides on the back of Mi-17 helicopters, swooping low over Afghan mountains in complete darkness, sitting on crates with nothing between me and the ground but a cargo strap. I would have missed out on long drives through rocky creek beds to avoid landmines, stopping on dusty roads to eat MRE rations, and rock-throwing contests with Afghan soldiers. I would have missed out on canoeing across the Chari River in the Sahara, water-skiing on the Congo, and shooting guns with the president of Yemen. I would have missed out on serving my country. Sure, I would have missed out on dysentery, danger, and other hardships, but I would have missed out on a lot of life. That is certain.

Foreword

Sometimes, becoming a man, or being one, is as simple as not switching lines. It is as simple as sticking to the mission.

I will not spew statistics at you, but let's look at just a few facts:

The number of men who are dating women is down, as are marriages, since men are marrying later and later.

Levels of satisfaction and happiness for the majority of those who do marry are down.

Employment participation rate is down.

Men's enrollment and graduation from college, even investing in a son's education and future, is down.[1]

While . . .

Obesity rates are up.

Consumption of pornography is up.

Video gaming is up.

Do you see any trend there? I do. I think that there are too many men who seem to be switching lines. Frankly, there are quite a few who seem to not even be lining up. I did not hope to write this book to reverse all of these trends. I know that there are no magical, miracle cures or secret CIA skills to fix all the problems. I wish that there were. But maybe my book can help.

---

1. See Hannah Rosin, "The End of Men," *The Huffington Post*, Sept. 13, 2012

1: BAD BOYS

I began my life as a bad boy. I admit that I was bad, despite what my mom thought of me and all her best efforts. You see, a mom sees the good in boys and little else. A dad, on the other hand, sees the bad and hopes for some good someday. Yep, dads know the truth. They know because they were bad boys too, when they were younger. Many still are.

I blame some of my badness—not all of it—on fire, or my attraction to it. Fire is as tempting as can be to a boy. Who hasn't sat next to a campfire, staring into the flames, hypnotized by the shifting shapes, the magic? Fire moves and flickers like a living, breathing creature, dancing along a wooden stage in multicolored costumes. It is chameleon-like as well, changing moods with each match, moving revelers with patriotic fireworks, thrilling an audience during a Vegas show, or warming children after a cold swim in the lake like a mother, drying their clothes and roasting their marshmallows.

Unfortunately, fire can also be a monster, a cruel tool of destruction. Boys can use it to destroy. Why a boy likes to destroy, I don't know. I just know that we do. Boys love blowing up mailboxes with M-80 firecrackers, chopping down trees, throwing rocks through windows of abandoned buildings, rolling boulders off thousand-foot cliffs, smashing bottles with rocks. Boys love to destroy; it seems to bring us joy.

Boys also love to shoot. What could be better than shooting a round from a high-powered rifle through a TV or microwave packed with Tannerite explosives? I'll tell you what could be better: shooting it with a grenade launcher, or a .50 caliber machine gun, or a Rocket Propelled Grenade (RPG), or a MANPAD (Man-Portable Air Defense System). Even that word, MANPAD, sounds manly. We love to shoot with larger and larger calibers, more rounds per minute, the bigger the better, overkill. That's why they call it *firepower*. To a boy, a rifle is the original joystick. Actually, to shoot is a hoot.

Boys love to crush: watermelons stolen from a farmer's field, vehicles in those huge car crushers at junkyards, monster trucks that drive over other vehicles, a bowling ball in a hydraulic press, an egg on a friend's head, or even a soda can on our own head. To crush is a rush.

But boys especially love fire, our favorite, trusted accomplice. We torch old timber mills during Boy Scout camps and watch the flames explode thirty feet in the air. We don't particularly love being scolded by the Scoutmaster, nor being ordered to sit at the "fireside" all night to ensure that the fire does not spread, but it's still worth it. We love matches, fire starters, lighters, torches, and even better—flamethrowers. My brothers and I fought over the GI Joe flamethrower action figure. Of course, a real flamethrower would have been even better, but they were hard to find for a boy of eight, fortunately. Yes, boys love to burn. Actually, we yearn to burn.

Okay, enough with the rhymes.

My love for fire was consummated, you might say, at an early age. One fine summer morning a friend of mine, Michael McFarren, confided that he had taken the key to a neighbor's home. The owners, the Dahls, had entrusted the key to Michael's parents, hoping they would care for the plants while they were away at Disneyland, and ignoring the fact that the McFarrens had a five-year-old pyromaniac son (is that redundant?) who played with a five-year-old pyromaniac friend, both of whom might try to burn their home to the ground. Did the thought that the Dahls were off vacationing in Disneyland, enjoying rides, hot dogs, and fluffy hotel towels, while we wandered our empty street with nothing to do, enter our juvenile minds and spur us to torch their home? Maybe. I don't recall any particular antipathy for them but merely sympathy for fire.

After we entered their home, we headed directly to the kitchen, where we searched the pantry. I first spotted saltine crackers on a shelf and grabbed the box. I have always loved saltine crackers, almost as much as fire. These were simpler times, before Cheez-Its; saltine crackers were the treat of the time. Michael and I tore into them like starving orphan boys, relishing our temporary independence and especially the freedom from nagging mothers: "Don't eat so fast," "Take one at a time," or "Close your mouth while you are chewing!"

As we laughed and chewed with our mouths wide open, I spied a box of wooden matches sitting on another shelf. These were not the wimpy restaurant matches, but wooden matches, matches to die for. They might as well have been calling to us from their package, "Yeah, baby, you see us! You remember us, the magic matches?! Let's do this!" Just as there was no mom to tell us to eat one cracker at a time, there was no mom to stop us from playing with those beautiful, voluptuous, wooden matches. Did I just say voluptuous? Well, that is how they looked to Michael and me at the time.

We quickly gathered up as many paper scraps, utility bills, cardboard pieces, and wooden objects as we could find and stacked them all in the center of the living room floor. We then each took a match, but as I lifted my match to strike it on the box, Michael grabbed me by the arm and said, "Wait! Let's make a star pattern on the carpet!" He then crouched down and arranged the pile, and more matches, in beautiful, delicate "rays" extending from the center outward. We then lit the fire. It wasn't long before the flames were melting the beautiful beige carpet and slowly spreading to the walls of the home. Destruction, yes, but with style.

As the fire grew, we began to dance around the flames in ecstasy, laughing, still stuffing our faces with crackers, spitting crumbs at each other. We were transported through time and transformed into cave boys, like our ancestors eons ago—eating, dancing, chanting, and burning. We were mesmerized by our creation, a glowing, magical pet that was slowly devouring the carpet and leaving a black, charred trail in its wake.

If we had not lit candles and placed them on the windowsills, my mother might not have found me. I imagine that the smoke billowing out the front door was also a clue to our whereabouts. Leaving the front door open was a fortunate mistake that ultimately cost us our pride but probably saved our lives. My mother soon had me by one ear, escorting me home on my tiptoes, most assuredly beginning to notice some signs of badness.

At age five, I was thinking only that my ear hurt, and that I needed to dispose of the rifle ammunition that I had found in Mr. Dahl's bedroom, next to his .30-06 hunting rifle. I had tried to load the gun during a break from the fire—which would have escalated our adventure, enabling us to burn, eat, and shoot at the same time—but eventually gave up and loaded my pockets instead. Even at five, I knew that I had to get rid of any evidence, so I stealthily dropped the finger-length rounds in front yards leading to our home. My mom did not notice a thing; I was that good, and that bad.

I suppose their insurance paid for the damage. I don't remember having to work it off, which would have taken years. I remember that the Dahls eventually forgave me. We even went on a family vacation together, camping with them at Arches National Park, near Moab, Utah. They did not put me in charge of the campfire. Burn me once, flame on you, burn me twice . . .

When I was not burning, I was flooding. Flooding can be loads of fun. Boys love a flood, with lots of mud. Okay, that's the last rhyme, I promise.

I'll tell you about flooding.

Our street, called Mandan Avenue—though it wasn't really an avenue at all—was the last outpost between suburban Salt Lake City streets and neighboring farms. Those of us unable to go to Disneyland (which meant most of the neighborhood) would often explore the nearby fields and trails, catch snakes, and play in the irrigation ditches. One ditch we visited regularly was affectionately called "Poop Creek," a half-misnomer since it was not much of a creek but did smell a lot like poop. It was located a bit farther away from home and, as one can surmise from the name, wasn't really worth the walk.

Snake Trail, which did have snakes, followed one of the ditches closer to our street and led to a small grove of poplars along the edge of a sugar beet field. To my friends and me, this field, which ran north and south along the eastern end of Mandan, served as playground, battleground, and highway to neighborhoods farther away. We regularly marched back and forth, cutting trail and not showing much concern for the beets.

All that crisscrossing through the field couldn't have done the beets much good. And that couldn't have made the farmer very happy—the farmer named Ramón.

We didn't know much about Ramón. We just knew that he was big. Everything about him was big, from his big cowboy boots to his big baby-blue Cadillac. We saw him on rare occasions when he would drive up to the edge of his field to check his beets—and do whatever beet farmers do—and then leave. Our childish imaginations filled in anything else we needed to know about Ramón: that he was meaner than a snake, and that if he saw you step on one of his beets, he would stick you in the trunk of his Cadillac, drive you out to the Salt Flats, stake you out on a red ant hill, and leave you to die. The very mention of Ramón's name sent shivers up our spines. He was the Mandan bogeyman.

One summer day, my friends David and Reuel and I did not have any matches and could therefore not burn anything, so we decided to dam up the ditch next to Snake Trail to make a swimming hole. It was hot and well before the days of swimming pools in every gated community, which our neighborhood was not. We gathered rocks, sticks, and mud—whatever we could find—and made our own pool, one that any beaver would have been proud to call his own. We were soon lying on our backs in the cool water, squinting up at the sunlight filtering through the leaves and discussing who was hotter: Ginger or Mary Ann, Veronica or Betty? And Jeannie? That was quite an outfit. I am sure that boys today have similar arguments, but with different contestants.

As we argued, two things escaped our attention, which often happens when boys discuss hotness. First, our beaver dam was too effective, and all that backed up water was overflowing out one side of our pool and pouring into the sugar beet field—the field of Ramón. Second, Ramón had decided to come to this field on this particular day, at this particular time, and had seen the water flooding his precious sugar beets. In fact, he was at this very instant driving his vehicle, the baby-blue Cadillac of Ramón, along the edge of the field, spinning his tires in the dirt, digging up his own beets. He was that mad.

The miracle of the human mind: drawing conclusions in split seconds. All three of our undeveloped but blossoming brains booted up in unison as we saw the Cadillac roll to a stop and Ramón's big boots appear beneath the door as he stepped out. We knew, as all beavers do, what a predator looks like. We exploded from the water in unison, jumped to our feet, and began to run. None of us spoke Spanish, but Ramón's words sounded like a swarm of angry bees as he ran toward us.

We wisely decided not to wait around for a translation and headed for home, which happened to be on the other side of his field.

At first, we tried not to step on his precious beets, but home was north and his rows ran east and west. Our strides were soon making salad of the tops of his beets. As we glanced back, we noticed that even Ramón did not appear concerned that his boots were also damaging crops since he followed our same route, slicing through the remaining plants that we hadn't damaged. We also noticed, with alarm, that he was surprisingly fast and agile in those big boots. And he was closing on us quickly. There is a joke about two men, walking on safari in the Serengeti, who spot a lion stalking them. One of them immediately sits down and begins to tie on his running shoes. His companion scoffs and remarks, "You're crazy if you think that you can run faster than a lion." The other chuckles and replies, "I don't have to run faster than the lion; I just have to run faster than you."

In hindsight, I don't think that any of us could have outrun that angry farmer, even in our adrenaline-induced panic. But I didn't have to run faster than Ramón—I just had to run faster than David. And on that fateful day in that sugar beet field, running from Ramón, we three friends learned the meaning of the expression, "every man for himself."

Don't get me wrong, as Ramón began to close in on David, and as bad a boy as I was, I did feel sorry for him. I even pictured David in my mind, a poor boy out in the Salt Flats, abandoned, thirsty, staked out on an anthill in his tighty-whiteys, calling for us in a weak, parched voice, "Help me." The thought was heartbreaking, as you might imagine. But I ignored the voice, of course, and kept running. I am sure that Reuel, who was not as bad as me, felt some compassion, but he didn't stop and wait for David either. I'm sure he had the same thought racing through his mind: "We can't save him, so why not put as much distance between David and ourselves as possible?"

Ramón picked David out of the herd, like any good predator, and began to close in. After a few rows, Ramón eventually caught up to David and kicked him in the seat of the pants with one of those huge boots. When boot connected with butt, David achieved liftoff. And that's when something amazing happened. Have you ever seen one of those long jumpers at a track meet, sprinting down the track, hitting that white board, springing into the air, and then continuing to run mid-flight, pumping arms and legs, defying gravity? David did that! He just kept pumping those chubby little legs, flailing his chubby little arms, and never missed a step when he landed a couple of beet rows later, both feet on the ground. That is most likely when the phrase "he hit the ground running" was born.

I think that Ramón must have been impressed with David's agility and distance, since he stopped chasing us—either that or he was satisfied that he had made contact. Regardless, Ramón shouted one last threat in Spanish as we disappeared into a backyard—which I have since translated: "If I ever catch you little gringos in my beet field again, I will hang you from a tree like a piñata at my next birthday and let my relatives beat you"—something to that effect.

I do not remember ever seeing Ramón after that, or making another dam, or ever playing anywhere near his sugar beets again. And I stopped burning homes, flooding fields, and blowing stuff up, except during those years in the CIA. If you are going to keep burning, flooding, blowing stuff up, and being bad as you grow older, then at least get paid for it.

2: STAND UP

Eventually, I did get paid to be bad. I joined the Central Intelligence Agency, the CIA. Interestingly, the CIA pays its operatives to lie, steal, cheat, evade the police, fight, and sometimes even blow stuff up. Imagine that. It is a bad boy's dream job.

In 1997, I found myself in Paris, France. It is a beautiful city—the city of lights, as they call it. I never dreamed that I would find it to be more a city of fights.

Before our arrival, I had noted in the State Department Post Report that we would be living in a very safe city with a low crime rate compared to other large metropolitan areas; the only significant threat to tourists, or foreigners living there, was from pickpockets prowling the subways and other tourist sites such as museums. By the year 2000, however, that safe climate had begun to change.

Although I often commuted on my bicycle, I usually rode the subway to and from meetings. One morning I stepped on a subway train, located a seat, and slipped into the state of semiconsciousness that overcomes most subway, subterranean travelers. Trains have always been relaxing to me, despite the crowds, and I can fall asleep if I let myself.

At the next stop I noticed a small group of people, including a rather stocky man in a large overcoat, enter our subway car. Although I wasn't paying much attention, I saw him out of the corner of my eye and noticed that he had stopped next to the exit. As the doors closed and the train began to move, he suddenly approached a passenger seated nearby and struck him with his fist—a roundhouse punch to the side of the head. The victim, a small-framed black man, had no warning and had not seen the attack coming. His head jerked violently to the right, and he slumped over in his seat toward the train window.

It's fascinating to note the emotions one feels when thrust into a situation like this. Government agencies, including the CIA, teach the psychology and science behind emotions that flood your system after witnessing violence, or becoming involved in that type of situation. A severe enough experience can release a "cocktail" of chemicals into a person's bloodstream, enough to shut him down and even immobilize him. Throughout history, many warriors screamed to further increase this shock during an attack. To defend against this shock, a person must quickly overcome the flood of emotions, focus on what is happening, decide what to do (fight or flight), and concentrate on survival.

Training, or muscle memory, will often help a person, especially during the initial moments of an attack. During this train assault, I experienced similar emotions: 1) surprise—*What the heck just happened?*; 2) shock—*How could that have happened in downtown Paris?*; to 3) anger—*I want to beat the heck out of the assailant.* All these emotions flashed past my eyes as fast as the walls of the tunnel flashed past our subway car. Without much thinking, I stood up and walked toward the attacker, who had now backed up against the train doors and folded his arms across his chest with a smug look on his face.

I asked the assailant, in French, why he had attacked the other commuter. He simply looked at me, scowled, and refused to answer. As you may have noticed above, my emotional train had come to a stop at *anger*. Still without thinking much, I grabbed him by his coat collar, shoved him against the doors, and asked him again why he had assaulted the other man. He again refused to respond and began to struggle with me, pushing me back and trying to loosen my grip.

At that point, I stepped back and pulled him with me, then tripped him to the floor of the train, where he landed on his hands and knees. He immediately reached out with one arm, attempting to grab one of my legs. I dodged and slammed a knee into the middle of his back, driving him to the floor. I then placed one of my shoes on his head. And that is where I found myself, standing there next to his prone figure, with a foot on his ear. I grabbed one of the straps hanging from a bar, to steady myself. And every time he tried to get up I simply twisted my foot and ground his ear into the floor. Don't ask me where I learned that move. But I did grow up the middle boy of three brothers and a younger sister—I need to ask them if I ever stood on their heads.

It was surreal. I remember looking around at the French passengers as the train shot through the tunnel, businessmen and women all dressed up for work and all now intently interested in their newspapers, novels, fingernails, or the insides of their eyelids. I'm sure that it couldn't have been easy to ignore a rather large man standing on another's head, and a third man lying on a bench, moaning. All this was happening just a few feet away from them, and there was no response, not even a sign that they had seen the violence.

As the train continued its route to the next stop, which seemed like an eternity, I wondered whether any of the passengers would eventually notice us or the moaning, injured victim lying down in his seat. Unfortunately, none seemed to notice during the ride, and none came to our aid.

Eventually, however, one young man did approach and suggested that we throw the attacker off the train at the next stop. I agreed and, understandably, expected him to lend a hand or foot. When we arrived at the next station, the train came to a stop and the doors slid open. I removed my foot from the thug's head, at which point he sprang to his feet, backed up against the opposite door, and raised his fists in the air to fight. I looked around for my would-be partner, or ring man, but he had now vanished. It was obvious that I was alone to handle the situation.

I first yelled at the attacker to get off the train, several times—nothing but more scowls. My blood began to boil again, as the bully refused to say a word, and still none of the other passengers had stepped forward to help me throw him off the train. Worse, no one would lift a finger to help the injured victim. Again without thinking—anger tends to empty your head of other thoughts—I rushed him, grabbed the lapels of his coat, and ran him out of the train. As we crossed the platform and approached the wall, I gave him an extra heave. His head made a loud thud, like a coconut on concrete, as he impacted the tiles, and he crumpled to the floor.

This is what the train conductor saw, since he had exited the train (one of the commuters had at least lifted a finger to pull the alarm) and was now walking back along the platform toward our car.

"What is going on?" he asked, in an alarmed voice. I quickly explained the situation and he appeared to believe me, especially when he noticed the injured man on the seat. I asked the conductor to call the police. "No, that is not my job," he replied, surprisingly. "I have to keep the train moving. Please escort the victim to the above-ground ticket booth for assistance."

I shrugged, entered the car, and helped the victim to his feet. As we exited the car, I noticed the thug had regained consciousness, stood up, run toward the front of the train, and entered another car. Needless to say, I was not about to leave the train with an innocent victim while this thug continued on his way. *Uh-uh, not gonna happen.*

I first struggled with how to explain the "not-gonna-happen" to the train conductor, calmly, clearly. And that can be difficult in a foreign language, in the heat of the moment. It can be frustrating, as well, to find a nuance in a foreign language. My French was fine, but I did not really know how to communicate the subtleties of a beat-down, like we have in English: *kick your butt, knock your teeth out, break your face,* or *clean your clock* (yes, guys used to say that). So, I turned to the conductor and, in my unrefined French, told him to get the attacker off his train before I drag him out and "kill him." Not so subtle.

The increasingly startled conductor raised his eyebrows and pleaded, "*Calme-toi, calme-toi,*" (calm down). He turned, rushed up the tracks, followed the attacker inside, and commanded him to leave the train. I put my arm around the poor African man, as he turned out to be, who now had a goose egg–sized bump on the side of his head, and escorted him up the station stairs to the ticket booth.

I wonder about all the alternate endings to this story—what could have been? The ticket booth attendant, who took our report, cautioned me against becoming involved in incidents in Le Metro, pointing out that the attacker could have had a knife. I have heard stories of Good Samaritans who are now dead. "*There but for the grace of God . . .*"

Would the other passengers have helped two victims? I think that we know the answer to that. The booth attendant had a point. I gave my name and address to the victim, in case he needed a witness at any trial, or for further help if he needed it.

A month or so later I received a letter from my new friend, an immigrant from Senegal. In his note, he thanked me for coming to his assistance. A couple of lines, written in somewhat broken French, read, "Thank you for helping me when others stayed seated. My head hurt a lot. But the bad man's head hurt worse than mine."

We are all faced with these kinds of decisions, to step in or step aside. Truthfully, I have not always made the right decision when it comes to stepping up for someone. I have to live with that. But this time, in this place, I stood up. I was not a bystander.

Guys, don't be a bystander when someone needs your help.

Don't stand idly by when someone is being bullied.

Don't stand by when your buddies speak disrespectfully about women or treat them poorly or abusively.

Don't leave your buddies to be staked out in their tighty-whiteys on an anthill in the Salt Flats.

But seriously, and I mean seriously, stand up for others when they need someone.

3: BANGED UP

O ur neighborhood was relatively new. The homes were new, the lawns were new, and the trees were all too young, flimsy, and fragile to hold a tree house. And boys need a tree house, or a hut, to escape parents, neighbors, chores, and girls. Mostly, they need a hut to get into trouble.

Since we did not have any grown trees, we decided to construct our hut in the rafters of our garage. We first scoured construction sites nearby for materials, scraped dried concrete off the scrap plywood, straightened nails with our hammers, and gathered carpet remnants. We pulled the boards up in the garage rafters for floors and walls. Our hut was soon furnished with rooms and wall-to-wall carpeting; the flooring was made up of many different colors, maybe, but it was luxurious nonetheless.

Soon, neighborhood boys found out about our hut and came visiting with posters and other decorations, even incense to burn. We nailed posters on the walls and strung hippie beads between the rooms. We installed reading lamps, powered by extension cords running up along the wall studs from an outlet. Honestly, they were more *looking* lamps, since they were not for reading. You see, we needed light to look at pornography. Isn't it odd that boys need a hut to hide from girls in order to look at girlie magazines?

***

Old Man Barker provided most of the girlie magazines. The Barkers were that family in many neighborhoods that had more cars on cinder blocks than wheels. Their front lawn was more dirt and dandelions than lawn. Their older son looked a lot like Scut Farkus, of *A Christmas Story:* red hair, freckles, and yellow teeth. I once saw him swerve in front of a car while he was riding down Mandan on his Stingray bicycle, a bike we all aspired to own: a dream bike with gooseneck handlebars and banana seat. Unfortunately, little Farkus Barker ended up pinned under the front bumper of the car, all tangled up in his bicycle. As we all crowded around to see the damage, I noticed a sticker on the seat that read, "Ground Beef." I pondered to myself, as I looked down at him, *What a strange sticker to have on a bike*, especially in his present condition.

He didn't die but was banged up. We boys were always getting banged up. This was before the Internet, which does not injure kids, at least not on the outside. We played in farm fields and canals, in dirt lots, on construction sites, climbing barbed wire fences (or "bob" wire as we called it), jumping the ditches, throwing dirt clods. At one point in my childhood, we lived across the street from the town hospital. At night we often rummaged through their dumpsters looking for used syringes, bottles of blood, or medicine, which we then injected into grasshoppers. We were real mad doctors. It was risky to us, that is for sure. I'm hoping to never run into a half-human, half-grasshopper creature, the result of our experiments.

While playing doctor was nice, blowing stuff up was still best. One hot summer day, David was lighting cherry bombs under tuna cans in the middle of the street, sending them rocketing into the air. Neighborhood kids crowded around and ran screaming as each firecracker was lit. After one particularly loud explosion, David looked down to see blood running from his wrist and down his fingers. The lid of the can had separated and sliced through the air and then through his wrist. He was fine after stitches.

Nowadays, boys just don't have as many opportunities to slit their wrists. We live in a safer, more protected, insulated, regulated society. Boys just don't have as many opportunities to get hurt.

A few years back, a church leader and good friend of mine asked one of our troop's twelve-year-old Scouts to hop in the back of my truck so we could travel from one campsite to another.

The young man looked up at us and asked, "How?"

"How what?" we asked.

"How do I get in the back of the truck?" the boy questioned.

My friend had to explain, "Put your hand on the top of the tail-gate, put your foot on the bumper, pull yourself up . . ."

I suppose that most boys no longer climb into the beds of trucks. Maybe that's a good thing. A friend of mine in first grade died when he fell off the tailgate of his dad's pick-up.

My mother must have thought that we looked for ways to hurt ourselves.

I could even jump bob wire, I thought, until I tried sneaking into a drive-in theater. One friend paid for a ticket and drove his parents' vehicle inside. The rest of us congregated in the sagebrush near the back fence, waiting for darkness. When we eventually decided the coast was clear, we sprinted toward the fence. I thought I could hurdle it, and I almost did. But the wire caught my lead leg, right under my knee, and tore my pants clear to my crotch. It left me with a mean gash along the back of my leg. I lost some pride. I could have lost a lot more, when you think about it.

Now there are no more drive-in theaters to give bad boys scars, or scarred thoughts or scarred memories.

When I first earned my driver's license, Reuel, David, Danny, and I decided to go see an R-rated movie at a drive-in. We had graduated from dirty magazines, and drive-in movies were just one more secret about which my parents knew nothing. We did not have enough money—as usual—and did not want to risk the barbed wire, so the three of them started arguing about who was the poorest and would hide in the trunk of my parents' Duster Twister. David won the argument and jumped in first. One block later, Reuel complained that it wasn't fair that David didn't have to pay, so I stopped and he got in the back. Before we arrived at the theatre, Danny also pleaded poverty, and convinced me to stop, again, for him to climb in the trunk.

When we reached the drive-in I drove up to the ticket window, alone. The lady asked me, "How many?" I thought, *That's a strange question*, but I realize, in hindsight, that maybe she had noticed the conspicuous tilt of the car, given all the weight in the back. I answered nervously, "One." I drove to the back of the drive-in and parked far away from the other cars. After a few minutes of listening to my friends pleading for me to let them out and banging on the trunk lid, I hurried to the rear, quickly opened the lock, and herded them quickly inside the car.

Not ten minutes into the movie, I was startled by a flashlight tapping on my driver's side window. "Tickets," the manager barked. When I could not produce the stubs, he marched us into the office, threatened to call the police, and warned us to never return. "Can we at least finish the movie?" David asked.

Granted, some kids can still find ways to hurt themselves. A Scoutmaster friend was chopping wood when a young boy volunteered to place the lengths of wood on the stump for him to split. Unfortunately, as one of the logs began to tip, the boy reached out to steady it—just as the Scoutmaster swung the ax. One chop, two fingers. Tip: don't help someone else chop wood.

I got hurt quite a bit. I was also hit by a car while riding my bike, just like Ground Beef Farkus. As I was rushing home from the city swimming pool one day, I pedaled across the intersection at Center and Main, but just as the light was changing. The car in the inner lane saw that I was late and waited, but a car heading south next to him did not and timed the green light so he would not have to slow down. I was hurled by the impact into the middle of the intersection. I still remember looking up from the hot pavement and seeing a lady on the sidewalk, in front of Woolworth's, put her hands to her face, just like the *Home Alone* boy, and let out a scream.

The screaming lady scared me more than being hit by the car. I quickly jumped up, grabbed my damaged bike, and started to ride again, one-legged, since my right knee hurt so bad, and because the right pedal was bent in so far that it scraped on the chain guard and made a "*chi-chunk, chi-chunk*" sound as I sped away. The driver first called after me to stop, then jumped back in his vehicle and motored after me. When he caught up with me a few stores down, he pleaded for me to stop, while asking if I was all right. I didn't stop, being too embarrassed, but yelled at him that I was fine. My right leg and hip hurt, and I had scrapes from the pavement, but I wasn't about to tell him that. When I think about it, the accident could have been worse—I could have had a *"Ground Beef"* sticker on my seat.

Other Mandan kids were hurt. One day a friend, Kyle, shot David's sister, Debbie, in the face with a BB gun. I don't think he did it on purpose. We all had BB guns. I shot David in the butt. David shot Reuel in the arm. Reuel shot Danny in the leg. It was like karma. BB's that go around come around. David's dad, whom we called Clyde the Legend, but not to his face, escorted Debbie outside and down the street, parading her around the neighborhood for all to see, like a live accident exhibit, crying her eyes out with the BB still embedded in the skin just below her nose. Clyde warned us all, as he dragged her along by the arm toward Kyle's home, the neighborhood children following like rats after the Pied Piper, "See what happens when you play with guns? Look at that! You see that? Look at that!"

We looked. We saw. *It's just a BB*, we all thought. We had all been shot. We all just snickered as we looked.

But we mostly looked at pornography in the hut. It's what boys will do, if you let them. Dads probably still don't think twice about leaving dirty magazines lying around in their closets. Dads might not worry because there is much worse on the Internet. And they take more care, I am sure, to safeguard their loaded guns. But why more concern for a loaded gun or matches than for pornography? To a young boy, pornography is just as dangerous. A gun just does the job a lot quicker.

4: SCHIZOPHRENIA

I've been told that we should not hate. We've all heard it: "Don't be hatin'!" But I do hate sometimes. I hate some things, like the scenes in Western movies of the sheriff setting a cattle rustler on a horse, placing a noose around his neck, and slapping the horse's flanks. The camera invariably pans to the victim's kicking feet, which twitch violently and eventually stop moving. I hate *Hang 'em High,* Clint Eastwood's movie. I hated "Hangman," the word game that we played during Sunday School when the teacher was absent. I even hate the lyrics from the "Hanging Tree" song in the *Hunger Games* books.

You might be wondering where all that hate for hanging comes from. I'll tell you where.

One afternoon, around the age of nine or ten, I walked out our back door and into the garage, for no apparent reason. Maybe I grew bored watching Skipper take off his hat to hit Gilligan for the umpteenth time. I don't remember. But as I opened the door and stepped inside, I looked across the room and saw Mark, my older brother, having hanged himself from a rafter. I remember every detail of the scene because that image was instantly burned into my mind like a hot branding iron. Sadly, I still have that image in my head, almost fifty years later. Some things cannot be unseen, like when you see your brother hanging from the rafters of a garage.

I immediately turned and ran, or stumbled, back into the house to call for help. As I rushed into the kitchen, I saw my mother standing by the stove, making dinner. She looked up at me, waiting for me to speak. I stood still. I tried with all my might to tell her what I had seen. I remember trying to formulate the words, get them out of my mouth somehow, but my brain and mouth had become disconnected, or short-circuited. Power surges in a home can overload a circuit and blow a fuse. My brain had obviously been overwhelmed with what I had seen. I could not talk or even breathe.

I sometimes have a dream that my mouth is filled with peanut butter, so full that I can't talk or even breathe, and I try to get the peanut butter out. I claw at it but can't get it out, and I choke and gag and try to call someone for help. That dream must be from that memory. That's exactly what it was like. Nearly fifty years later I can still feel it, the frustration and guilt of not being able to talk or shout or even bark. Even Lassie, the hero collie dog, would bark to warn of danger. I just stood there. I was experiencing that chemical cocktail dump in my system.

My mother asked me what was wrong but quickly realized by my look of shock that something terrible had happened and rushed past me, out the door to the garage. Seconds later I heard her scream for my father. As my dad rushed outside, I followed in a trance, watching as they struggled to hold Mark up so my dad could untie the knot. Once the rope was released they carefully laid him on the concrete floor, unconscious. It took all of my self-control to not vomit.

No boy, no matter how bad, no matter how many living rooms burned, mailboxes blown up, or fields flooded, should have to see that. I didn't deserve that. I know that now.

What came after was a blur: ambulance, hospital, coma, hushed conversations at home, neighbors huddled in front yards, cruel comments from classmates, desperate prayers at my mother's bedside. Mark remained in a coma for several days but he survived. A scar on his throat near his Adam's apple, from a tracheotomy, was eventually the only outward sign of what had happened to him.

Our family scars might not have been visible but they were deeper. There were no grief counselors, doctors, or therapists, not any of them for any of us. And we needed counseling more than Mark did, I am convinced. He certainly did not appear as traumatized as we were. He did not see himself hanging from the garage rafters. He did not have to close his eyes, tight, for countless nights, for years, trying to block that image, to somehow squeeze it out of his mind. He did not listen to his mother crying for weeks, months, eventually years. He did not have to defend himself from whispering neighbors who boasted that they knew the real story, that it wasn't an accident, that Mark had actually wanted to kill himself because he had been abused or was high on drugs, or just for the thrill.

There were lots of whispers in those days, especially around us children. Maybe that is one sign of the growth of a society. During stage one of societal evolution, unpleasant things are left unspoken. Stage two, gossip is whispered. Stage three, anything, no matter how vulgar, is discussed openly, even shouted for all to hear. Let's call it societal devolution instead.

In those days, we lived in stage two, the whispering stage. Parents would whisper about goings-on in the neighborhood, about swear words, drugs, or sex. About marital problems. Parents tried to protect us, of course, to protect our souls. But children have excellent ears. And we knew, as all children do, that whispered information is the best. When we heard their whispers we pressed them to reveal more.

But I did not want to hear the whisperings about Mark. I knew that the whisperings were not true. I knew that Mark had not been abused, so it must have been an accident. And I stuck with the accident story supplied by my well-meaning parents, explaining that he had slipped; yes, that is what had happened. He was using the rope to pull more boards up into our hut, yes, and had lost his balance and slipped, the rope reaching out somehow and tangling around his neck, yes. I believed it, even when no one else in the neighborhood did, I am sure, but that is the story my parents gave us, so I stuck with it, hoping that it was true.

I stuck to the story even when Mark threatened to beat me up—or actually did. I stuck with it when he slammed my foot in the door of our old station wagon, breaking it. I stuck with the story as I learned to hate him.

I stuck with the story when Mark fought an older neighbor boy, and I wanted so bad to help him, screaming at the top of my lungs for that long-haired hippie to leave Mark alone, even while I hated him for what he was doing to us. I continued to stick with the story when he came home drunk or high on drugs, cursing my parents, threatening them, fighting my dad in the hallway while my sister and younger brother listened from our beds, acting like we were asleep, trying to be asleep to not hear the chaos.

No one ever told me, but I eventually figured it out. Mark had not slipped. Ropes are not magic. He had purposely tied it around his own neck. He had tried to kill himself.

Mark slowly faded into a world of delusion, anger, violence, and schizophrenia. He no longer remembers that day in the garage, nor trying to kill himself other times. He does not know that he hanged himself again years later, on my birthday, and that I cleaned up the blood where he fell and hit his head when the rope snapped from his weight, fortunately. Maybe.

What if I had decided to watch Skipper smack Gilligan one more time before I went to the garage, or my dad had not found him in that same garage with a hose leading from the exhaust to his open window? Then Mark would not have been around to torture my tortured parents for another forty years. He would not have been around to fight with my younger brother or bully my younger sister. He would not have been around to embarrass us at Boy Scout camps, family outings, meals, reunions, weddings, and funerals. He would not have been around. And we could have laid flowers on his grave and cried once a year, maybe more, but not every day.

But that's not how life works. We don't get to choose what others do, when others fall ill, when others leave this life. We can't even choose when we go, or at least we shouldn't. We can only choose to control those things we can control, and how we react to the rest, particularly to what life throws at us, and then make the best of it.

5: SHIH TZU-PHRENIA

There's something else that I hate, besides schizophrenia. Let's call it Shih Tzu-phrenia.

You've probably never heard of this condition. I first encountered Shih Tzu-phrenia, a relatively new illness and one that I discovered and named, in Brussels, Belgium, while visiting my wife's aunt, Tontine Marie José. She was a nice lady who did not come across at all like my brother. She did not threaten me, punch me in the face, hang tinfoil from the windows, or paint the television screen like Mark did. She did, however, have a Shih Tzu.

I have nothing against pet owners. I have had pets. My first pet, an orange tiger cat, which we so aptly named Tiger, was a fine pet, until my parents found it dead, hanging from the top of the chain-link fence in our backyard. Our luck wasn't much better with our family of gerbils.

But I enjoyed our pets just the same.

Tontine Marie José did too, but more than most people. During our visit to her home in the outskirts of Brussels, her Shih Tzu strolled into the room like he owned the place, plopped down in the middle of the room, and began licking his privates. I glanced around to see if anyone else noticed. My wife was busy talking and did not seem to notice the distraction. Maybe she was like most people in polite company—in a first stage society—that leave things unsaid, or do not let on that they notice, like passengers in a subway train. I looked to Tontine, somewhat desperate, hoping that she would shoo the dog away, but she didn't seem to notice the dog either. I'll tell you something, Lassie knew how to call for help, and Lassie never licked herself. Ever.

To my horror, when the mutt was finished, he hopped up on Tontine's lap, placed a paw on each shoulder, and began licking her face. I gasped in shock. Granted, I could have said something to stop it. But I did not feel it was my place to tell an older lady how to treat her dog.

I looked on hopelessly as Tontine proceeded to return the kisses, accompanied by affectionate expressions of "coochie-coochie coo."

Many Europeans, including Belgians, kiss a lot. They kiss you when you arrive; they kiss you when you leave. In France, casual acquaintances receive two kisses on the cheeks, while close friends and family receive four. In Belgium, it is one or three. As I watched Tontine kiss her dog, the thought struck me, like a cold shower, that I would receive three kisses; all those doggy germs were coming my way.

I tried not to think about it during the rest of the visit. I closed my eyes tight, trying to remove another burned image from my brain. *Maybe she will forget to kiss me when I leave. If I stand up straight she can't reach my face. What if I do one of those Hollywood "air" kisses, like you see at the Academy Award parties?*

My fears were well founded. She kissed me on both cheeks. One more memory to erase.

In many parts of the world, people do not look at pets with the same level of affection. In America, for example, Bun Bun the rabbit is well cared for, fed, bathed, and smothered with affection. In Greece, rabbits are well-done, bathed in a wine sauce, and smothered in onions. In Belgium, dogs are part of the family. In other parts of the world, they are part of the menu.

I was a missionary on the island of Rarotonga, in the Cook Islands, and once visited a friend named Kimi. While we are talking, Kimi's six-year-old son came running up to report that their dog had killed and eaten one of their chickens. Kimi casually asked the boy to bring the dog. My missionary companion and I give each other a look like, *Uh-oh, that dog is in trouble.* But curiously, Kimi did not appear angry or even upset while we waited.

Not long after, the boy returned, leading the dog on a rope leash. As Kimi continued talking to us, he took the end of the leash and threw it over the limb of a nearby tree, hanging the dog. *Oh, I guess he will just choke it a bit,* I thought, cringing inside. Kimi then tied the rope with a knot. *Maybe he is really going to punish it, then let him down,* I hoped. But before I could say a word, Kimi beat the dog to death with a club and prepared its meat for a meal later that day, all the while chatting about the weather, fishing, and general island news.

People in many areas of the world consider dogs a part of the food chain, below us. Starting from the bottom, grass is eaten by grasshoppers, which are eaten by chickens, chickens eaten by dogs, and dogs by Kimi. And since dogs are not considered part of the family, Kimi does not consider himself a cannibal.

I met a diplomat in Europe who was a Shih Tzu-phrenic, you might say, and no longer occupied the highest link in the food chain with Kimi. He had a pet, a black dog whose original name was Buckwheat. The diplomat diplomatically renamed the mutt "Mr. Wheat." The diplomat loved Mr. Wheat. His office was full of framed photos of Mr. Wheat—the diplomat with his arm around Mr. Wheat, the diplomat and Mr. Wheat frolicking in the wildflowers in the hills above the city, the diplomat and Mr. Wheat welcoming visiting dignitaries. The photos were on the walls, the desk, everywhere. Interestingly there were no photos of the diplomat's wife or human children.

Sadly, the diplomat granted Mr. Wheat unlimited access. The diplomat even ordered the guards to issue Mr. Wheat a security badge, complete with a photo. Mr. Wheat galloped through the offices and hallways like he owned the place. He mingled at parties. He swam in the diplomat's pool, which was closed to other families. Mr. Wheat reigned supreme.

The diplomat traveled frequently and one day decided to spend some hard-earned taxpayer dollars for a trip to some of the religious sites in the country. One monastery invited the diplomat to stay overnight, which is an honor. Sadly, as the diplomat and staff proceeded to enter the monastery grounds with Buckwheat in tow, the monastery staff advised that dogs—and curiously, women—were not allowed inside, and neither had set foot in the monastery walls for a thousand years or more. The diplomat was highly offended and argued with the monks, who would just not allow Mr. Wheat inside. Angry at the snub, the diplomat left the monastery compound in a huff, deciding instead to sleep outside the monastery walls with his dog.

Sadly again, tragedy struck toward the end of his tour. One morning, the diplomat was walking Mr. Wheat around the compound grounds, which had been undergoing landscaping and renovations. Mr. Wheat chose to relieve himself near the fence (by the way, I have two sons, neither of whom I would allow to wee-wee on an fence in public). Unfortunately, the dog went wee-wee on an exposed, live electrical wire that was protruding from an unfinished lighting fixture. Mr. Wheat expired, in what must have been a painful jolt and despite the diplomat's desperate attempts at mouth-to-snout resuscitation.

I find myself asking a couple of questions all these years later: had Mr. Wheat just finished licking his privates before frying them? If yes, would the diplomat still have performed mouth-to-snout on Mr. Wheat? And finally, what would Kimi have possibly thought if he had happened upon the scene and witnessed the diplomat blowing into Mr. Wheat? *I'll be right back with my rope and knife.*

A few days later, a group of sympathetic employees were huddled outside the cafeteria, mourning the loss of Toasted Wheat—yes, I renamed him—who had already been buried on the grounds. I walked up, listened for a while, and then volunteered that it was sad indeed, "So sad that all that meat, freshly smoked, went to waste." Yes, I said that, unfortunately.

Now, these employees might hate me for saying that. I would tell them, *don't be hatin'.* I didn't hate Toasted Wheat. As a matter of fact, I still enjoy toasted wheat bread with bacon and eggs. I just don't believe that we can't settle for something in between obsession and hate when it comes to our pets.

6: KOREAN CROTCH SHOT

One of those countries with dog on the menu is South Korea, but less so over the years. To tell you the truth, I ate some of the best food of my life in South Korea. My favorite local dish is called beef bulgogi; it is prepared with a special, sweet sauce. In many Korean restaurants, each table has a grill where customers can prepare the meat to their own satisfaction. It is wonderful, much better than the sea slugs—which I hate—that we ate at another restaurant.

During the late 1980s, I found myself in Seoul, the capital of South Korea. I loved the country, especially for their meat. Guys love meat. A friend of mine owns a restaurant that specializes in salads. Most days, ninety percent of his customers are women. He talks about offering more meat on the menu, to attract more male clientele. I wonder what he is waiting for.

After work hours, we often shopped in a suburb of Seoul called Itaewon. The area was full of shops, most of which sold counterfeit items: fake brand-name sneakers, neckties, handbags—all knock offs. I've always had a hard time finding size fifteen shoes. When I found some my size in Itaewon, I bought several pairs.

One afternoon after work we visited a Korean special forces camp. There was a variety of training taking place at a camp next to us: rappelling down concrete buildings—sometimes upside down—room breaching, firearms training, martial arts, and even knife-throwing. It was entertaining to watch: lots of men in black fatigues running around, jumping off structures, fighting, and creating explosions. Basically, destroying stuff.

As we were walking to our vehicles, our interpreter took us near the group of knife-throwers so we could watch them train, impaling long throwing knives into wooden targets. I don't know of anything that could have made a group of guys happier—eating lots of meat, blowing stuff up, *and* knife-throwing. We enjoyed the show until the commander of the ROK (Republic of Korea) military unit approached our group, introduced himself, and asked if one of us would like to take a turn with a knife. We all glanced at each other and shrugged. Of course, my two companions both volunteered me.

The commander called one of the soldiers to bring me a knife, which appeared to be about a foot long and double edged. His unit all stopped their training and gathered around to watch. I took the knife by the blade and lined myself up in front of a target, which was probably twenty yards away. The target had a human figure, about five feet tall, painted on the front.

I was nervous, to put it mildly. I have always had a good arm but did not have much hope of sinking the knife in the target. I just knew that I had to make a respectable toss. As approximately one hundred Korean special forces soldiers looked on, waiting for the "round-eye" to fail, I hefted the knife, took aim, and let it fly. All our eyes watched as it spun and sliced through the air. Miraculously, the knife blade somehow rotated just right and stuck perfectly, deep into the board. And, as luck would have it, I had hit the human figure right in the crotch. A perfect throw.

The reaction was immediate. All one hundred privates instantly bent over and grabbed their privates, cringing, and then jumped in the air, applauding in unison, cheering and laughing. They did not lift me on their shoulders, but almost. Handshakes and pats on the back followed. The commander congratulated me on the throw.

As all men know, it was the perfect throw. To men, to soldiers, a crotch shot trumps a head shot any day. To men, Korean or American or Russian or any nationality, a crotch shot is magic, even money. Movie directors know it. I am certain that every comedy director either plans one gratuitous crotch shot for every movie or suggests it when they find a lull in the action or plot— "How about a crotch shot?" Funny video shows on TV are filled with crotch shots. There are YouTube videos of the top ten best crotch shots, dodge ball crotch shot videos that first show the clip forwards, then in reverse, in slow motion, then slow-motion reverse. There are countless videos of guys punching each other between the legs with the typical ending. The victim invariably crumbles to the ground while all of his friends collapse in laughter. Soccer ball to the crotch, golf ball to the crotch, little boy's baseball bat to Dad's crotch. It is hilarious, no matter how many times we see it. Slapstick, slap-crotch humor.

What is it about guys and a crotch shot, anyway? Is it the word? It does sound funny, I'll admit. *Crotch, crotch, crotch.* But we have all been kicked or punched in the crotch, or fallen on a fence with one leg dangling on each side, and lain on the ground for a long time, hoping the pain will subside, trying not to throw up. It is awful. We all know that it hurts worse than about anything. Yet it is funnier than anything when it happens to someone else. Ah, that is the key.

Fortunately, I had represented our team, the CIA, and even our country, with that one knife throw. Call it a crotch shot for international relations. That one event probably did more for the relations between our two countries than all our efforts to swallow sea slugs in their fancy restaurant.

Enough about crotches. There are times in all of our lives when we are thrown into the spotlight or into situations where we might fail—miserably—with hundreds of troops laughing at us rather than applauding. So what. That's life. And it will still be a great story— eventually. Just take a chance. Step up and throw.

7: CONCRETE AND MAIN STREET

My childhood wasn't all bad. I have good memories too. And a big part of my good memories include Sally and Beth.

I spent several of my summers in a small town that offered a city pool at the city park, just off Main Street, of course. The pool was the highlight of our summer. I spent all day, practically every day, of every summer of my childhood, at that pool. At times we would wander out into the hills or desert surrounding our town to catch lizards or scorpions, which we would watch fight in my mother's washtub. But the heat would eventually drive us to the pool.

I loved that swimming pool. It was a refuge from the desert and from summer boredom. But mostly I loved that pool because it was where Sally and Beth worked. They were the most beautiful lifeguards in the world, and hotter than the desert.

Sally worked in the office and Beth was the lifeguard. Both were stunning, one a blonde and one a brunette—bookends of beauty. They pushed out other contestants in our hotness arguments—Ginger and Mary Ann, Jeannie . . . Elly May. Did I mention Elly May, of *The Beverly Hillbillies*? Back to Sally and Beth. They were stunning. Of course, while we swam and splashed and learned tricks off the diving board we sometimes forgot about them. But when we were lying on that hot concrete surrounding the pool during breaks, they were *who* we thought of, they were *what* we thought of, they were *all* we thought of.

Thinking about it now, I should credit Sally and Beth with teaching me to swim. We enjoyed swimming, sure, but not for five hours a day, rain or shine, until the sun went down. Who knows, if it hadn't been for them, I might have eventually drowned during that canoe trip on the Snake River or spearfishing off Pounders Beach in Hawaii years later. They probably saved my life because, for a twelve-year-old boy, those two girls provided all the motivation, inspiration, and perspiration we needed, all wrapped up in a swimsuit.

I usually rode my bike home from the pool, heading south on Main Street, checking the phone booths for forgotten change. A nickel or dime in the coin slot usually meant a bottle of orange Nehi at the auto parts store. When we couldn't find change, we looked for soda bottles to turn in for a nickel. I can't imagine how many miles of roadsides I searched for discarded bottles. I scoured dumps and backyards and even asked neighbors for any "extra" bottles. I wanted empty bottles so bad that I sometimes bought a soda for a dime, just so I could turn in the bottle for a nickel. I know that doesn't make much economic sense, but I don't feel that stupid. "Grown-ups" do it today, spending thousands to get a tax return of hundreds at the end of the year.

One day I raced up Main Street to my favorite phone. As I propped my bike against the booth, I noticed a large briefcase sitting on the ledge below the phone. I looked around for the owner, but there was no one nearby. I don't know that I really thought much about it, but I just grabbed it and took it to the police station around the corner. They took my name and thanked me for dropping it off.

About an hour after arriving home, I heard a knock at the door. Mom called me to the front room where a man was standing with a briefcase in his hand. He told me that his "whole life" was in that briefcase that I had found and thanked me for being honest and turning it in to the police. He then held out a ten-dollar bill and offered it to me as a reward. My mom told me to take it, and we thanked him in return. To a young boy in the late 1960s, that ten dollars was a small fortune.

That might have been the first time that I had any money to speak of. I soon decided that I wanted more, and I started my own business—selling worms to fishermen. Actually, they were not just worms, but night crawlers, which are bigger, longer, and fatter than regular worms, guaranteed to catch bigger, fatter fish; this was way before the days of PowerBait. I posted a sign on the tree out front of our house, "Night crawlers 25 cents a dozen," and waited for the money to roll in.

It was harder than I thought. I had to water our lawns and then wait until late at night, creeping around and snatching the worms before they could slip back into their holes. I eventually obtained a "shocker," an electric probe that I would stick into the ground to shock the worms out. This "worm prod" didn't seem to help my sales all that much. I soon tired of worms, bottles, and coin slots, and figured that I would just look for more briefcases.

I ended up working at a few stores on Main Street when I was older. I worked in a clothing store but don't remember selling very many clothes. I don't think anyone had much money, and they were probably out checking phone booths. I spent much of the time waiting for customers, watching pedestrians and Mr. Hoyle. Mr. Hoyle was an insurance salesman in town, and a good one. But like many successful businessmen, and professional baseball players, he was a bit superstitious, or eccentric.

We watched his daily routine with fascination. At 4:50 p.m. sharp he would walk east across Main Street, enter the post office, check his mail box, return to the front entrance and peer out, return to his box (to see if they had added a letter or two in the previous five seconds), return to the door, exit, walk down the steps to the sidewalk, hop back up one step backwards, place his hands on the handrail, gaze north up Main Street, return to his car, get in, get out, get in, and leave. That was his daily pattern, without fail. Those were his impulses, which he could not, or would not, control.

We watched it day after day. I have always been fascinated by quirks. I must have a few, but I suppose we don't notice our own. Anyway, an idle mind is the devil's workshop, as they say. During one particularly boring day, I noticed a kid from the neighborhood walking by. I grabbed him by the arm and told him that I'd give him a candy bar if he would go over and sit on the handrail after Mr. Hoyle had entered the post office.

We waited until our victim arrived on the scene, and I sent the boy running across the street. He sat on the rail, exactly where I told him, and exactly where Mr. Hoyle would stop, place his hands, and gaze northward. Not a minute later we saw Mr. Hoyle's face at the window. Yep, there he was, right on cue. A minute later, another look. Then another. And another. Even from across the street we could see the panic starting to set in.

After ten or more minutes we realized that Mr. Hoyle was not about to leave that post office, which had now closed for the day. I felt guilty for my prank and whistled at the boy to return; he jumped off his perch and raced back across the street to us. Mr. Hoyle immediately exited, running down the steps as fast as he could. He quickly did his jig, placed his hands on the rail, gazed up the street, and raced to his car.

I didn't work very long at that clothing store. I probably wasn't very good in customer relations. Maybe I didn't pay good enough attention. One day a nurse who had treated me at the hospital, when I had injured my knee, walked into the store. I looked at her and she looked at me, both knowing that we were acquainted but not remembering when or where we had met. She remembered first and exclaimed, "Oh, I remember, you were my patient at the hospital. I just didn't recognize you with your clothes on."

The Fourth of July was the highlight of the summer. We watched many parades from the front steps of that old post office on Main Street. During our younger years we bought bags of peas, which came with a free peashooter tube to shoot at floats and people in the parade. Imagine that! We can't remember putting anyone's eye out. The Fourth of July meant races at the park, fishing booths, dunking ponds, snow cones, and greased pig competitions. A pig was covered with grease and released in a pen, where a hundred or so kids would try to catch it. First one to catch it got to keep it. I dreamt of catching that pig, when I wasn't dreaming of Sally and Beth.

Another competition was the grease pole, and it was just that—a pole that was greased from top to bottom. Anyone able to climb it could grab the ten-dollar bill at the top. We covered ourselves with dirt and sand in a desperate attempt to get some traction, which didn't work. Nothing we did seemed to work until we made a human pyramid, and the lucky kid at the top got the money. The rest of us went home with nothing, covered in grease and dirt. It was clearer and clearer to me that finding lost briefcases was still the best means to making money.

I eventually graduated from hunting coins, bottles, briefcases, and scorpions, to hunting girls on Main Street. There was no Internet, video games, discos, iPods, Wiis—there was just Main Street. On Friday nights we would "drag Main" for hours, up and down, hoping to meet girls, with not much success. The route was south on Main, through two traffic lights, left turn at the Dairy Freeze, through the parking lot, quick glance inside to see if anyone had stopped inside, north on Main, through two traffic lights, right turn into Hermie's, circle the lot, glance inside to see if anyone had stopped there, back south again, turn, back north again, for hours. I drove it so much that I could still do it in my sleep. We'd occasionally spot some cute girls in a car, give chase, catch them, not know what to do once we caught them, drive past, and slug the driver for going by too fast, and he would then slug us back for not talking when we had the chance.

I still love Main Street. The pool is long closed down, bulldozed, and replaced by a library. There are no more phone booths. You can't find a peashooter salesman anywhere. And Mr. Hoyle passed away a few years back. But Main Street is still there, and the old post office. When I think about it not much has changed, including me. I still like to swim, lie on hot concrete next to a swimming pool, and look at my wife.

8: LATE NIGHT FOOD FIGHT

I've always found it fascinating that most higher principles or doctrines that we study—such as political science, psychology, or diplomacy—apply just as accurately, and predictably, to situations in the playground as they do in "grown-up" conflicts. While teaching small children, I have seen them perform manipulation and elicitation ploys on their targets, surveillance on their opponents, and counterterrorism in games like dodgeball, all sometimes executed better than operatives in espionage. The same goes for principles of war. Children learn at a very early age how to win a war. And quite often a childish conflict follows a natural escalation, just as it does in a fight, a war, or a grocery store.

My first job was at an Albertson's grocery store, at the age of fifteen. I was hired to stock shelves—usually from around 9:00 p.m. until 5:00 or 6:00 a.m. The job consisted of unloading cases of goods—cans, boxes, bottles—from the large 18-wheelers at the back dock, wheeling the cases to the correct aisle with a dolly, cutting open the cases and stocking, and then aligning, or "facing," the shelves. It was boring, tedious work. And I suppose, in my attempt to excuse my bad behavior, that any fifteen-year-old would be tempted to misbehave.

To our credit, most nights my coworker friends and I were focused on getting the job done and done right. We often worked in a fury during the first few hours, hoping to complete the night's work early. I learned to run a stack of cases down an aisle, drop it off, and ride the dolly to the back room with very little effort and a great deal of speed.

Granted, there was more than one broken bottle of dill pickles, but we usually were able to finish the eight-hour job in around half that time.

Sadly, I can't say that our motives for finishing the job were pure. We knew that finishing early would give us time to relax. Even better, we would have time to goof off. Goofing off then evolved into teasing each other, and teasing evolved into full-fledged food fights.

There's nothing like a good food fight. Even at fifty-seven years old I would still love to be in a good old-fashioned food fight. I look at the food fight in the movie *Animal House*, instigated so cleverly by John Belushi, as the pinnacle of food fighting, good vs. evil, nerd against cocky jock, jello vs. crème brûlée. Food fighting is probably as ancient as civilization itself—and it is a dying art. Why is there no amusement park or food fight festival? I suppose it is obvious. It wouldn't be any fun if it were allowed.

That particular Albertson's grocery store did not allow food fights. I am sure that it was my friend—let's call him John, in honor of John Blutarsky (of *Animal House*)—who started the war by lobbing a box of cereal from the neighboring aisle. Oh, it's all fun until someone puts an eye out. Okay, I didn't lose an eye, but getting hit in the head with a box of Wheat Chex can leave a mark. I remember reaching for marshmallows but quickly realized that was not an effective weapon. I countered by rolling sixteen-ounce cans of pork and beans down the aisle at him—bean bowling, you might call it. He was easily able to avoid single cans until I sent more, going "full auto" with several rounds, or cans, at him in quick succession. He tried to jump them but landed on one and sprained his ankle.

The conflict continued to escalate through other grocery items and into whipping cream. There is nothing funnier than someone with a face full of cream, either whipping or shaving. Grown adults—professional baseball players, mostly—relish the idea of throwing a pan full of shaving cream into their teammate's face while he's being interviewed on national television. There is nothing funnier to a man deep down in his funny bone—except maybe the crotch shot.

At one point in our most heated battle—around 3:00 a.m.—John was hiding in the produce section and peering out the plexiglass window on the swinging doors. He could not see me, crouched beneath the window, waiting for him to exit. He finally peeked out and received the full blast of whipping cream directly in the face. It was glorious. His entire face was completely covered—white as a ghost.

It is fun to laugh so hard that you can't run, or hardly walk, or breathe, and almost pee your pants. I wish that I could laugh that hard every day. Like I said, I need to get in more food fights.

After this particular salvo, I barely managed to limp away, laughing till my insides hurt trying to breathe. I knew that I would have a minute or two to escape while he wiped the cream off, out of his eyes and mouth. I ran into the back area of the grocery department, into the men's restroom. I would be safe here. He would never think to look for me there. *He will not even be able to see out of those red eyes of his, stinging, crying, that little crybaby! Oh my gosh, I have to stop laughing or he will find me! Shut up, you fool! But did you see that white face with little bumps where his glasses used to be? Bwaahhh! Stop it, hide!*

But there is something odd that happens when you enter a bathroom. It seems to trigger a primeval urge to "go." Why else would someone who is in the middle of a battle decide to "go"? How stupid is that? And how much more stupid is it to go "number two" during a major conflict—the most critical battle to date in Albertson's. In my defense, it is difficult to think straight at fifteen, working at a grocery store unsupervised, in the heat of a vicious food fight at three o'clock in the morning.

I chose a stall and a magazine and sat down to wait out the conflict. Just let things calm down a bit. Détente. Mutually assured destruction. *Why does he insist on these juvenile battles, anyway? Why can't we settle this in a civilized manner, using diplomacy, understanding? Why can't we just all get along?*

A good friend of mine from college and a fellow student who interned with me in Washington, DC, told me that his assignment in the US Congress was so dreadfully boring that he would often sneak into the men's bathroom, find an empty stall, and take naps on the toilet. He got so he could sleep an hour at a time. I wonder how many of our senators and congressmen have adopted that practice. Maybe it wouldn't be a bad thing.

Just as I was finishing and getting ready to exit the bathroom, still reveling in my successful attack, I was jolted awake. I looked down at my feet and saw nothing but orange fire swallowing my legs. It wasn't like the beautiful, delicate, dancing fire on the Dahls' living room rug, or the "comforting mother" type. This was the "monster" kind, a scorching torch shooting under the stall from a can of hairspray, held by a laughing John. Bursts of hot orange flames seared my calves and instantly singed the hairs off my fifteen-year-old legs—hairs I had been carefully cultivating for the past few years. If the walls had been any higher, I would have lost more than the hair.

I quickly pulled my pants up and exited the stall. I saw John, who was now limping through the store, laughing so hard that he could not run, nor walk, trying to breathe from laughter. I limped after him and congratulated him on his stealth; he congratulated me on my marksmanship. There were no hard feelings. Some of the hair has even grown back.

9: TIME TO LIE

People lie. Some people lie a lot. I was paid to lie during my years in the CIA. In high school, I did it for free.

My senior year in high school was stressful. High school is hard enough when you have plenty of friends and worse when you don't. Unfortunately for me, my family had moved from Salt Lake City to a small town in 1975, the summer before my senior year, so I was short on friends. I didn't know anyone, other than a few kids I had met during summers spent there; I felt every bit the outsider, the "new guy," when I showed up the first day of school.

I tried out for football in the fall, mainly at my father's urging. I had played my sophomore year up north but wasn't much good and didn't play much. Fortunately, I had grown a few inches, put on a few pounds, and gained a little speed—very little—in the intervening years. Coach Bishop must have seen something in me because I made the team and eventually the starting defense. He encouraged me to work hard on the field and made me feel a part of the team. I will always appreciate his giving me a chance.

As the season progressed, I began to make new friends and started to feel like I might fit in after all. Near the end of our season we ran up against a very tough team, Davis High School. Davis is located at the other end of the state, near Salt Lake City. Long bus rides were a part of life in those days—our closest regional rival was a good fifty miles away. The bus ride to Davis was a little less than 300 miles—around six hours on a bus.

B. D. Foley

There's not much to do during bus rides. Once you have sung "99 Bottles of Beer on the Wall" you are left with stupid games, jokes, drinking soda pops, talk about girls, more sodas, more jokes, more sodas. I-15 is a long, desolate, empty desert road that splits Utah from north to south. There might be one rest stop, and the bus driver wouldn't stop, especially for a player who had drunk too many sodas.

Halfway through our trip, our quarterback, Scott, had drunk too many sodas and was practically rolling in the aisles in pain. He was also very competitive, and he claimed that he could pee longer than anyone else. We all said, "Prove it." The bus finally stopped to gas up, and we followed Scott to the restroom. He spouted for one minute and five seconds. I'm not sure how I still remember how long Scott peed, nor what the other travelers in the bathroom were thinking when they saw a group of guys crowded around Scott's urinal, checking their watches and cheering. To his credit, Scott ended up with both football passing and peeing records for the school.

We played a great game against Davis High School and had a chance to win, but we ran out of steam. One last drive by them and a dropped pass by us in the end zone was the difference. Funny how small, seemingly insignificant events—a missed block, a missed tackle, a missed flight—often make all the difference in life. Each starts a series of events, a sequence. And the clock runs out. And lives are changed, forever.

The entire team was distraught after the game; our team captain sat in the corner of the locker room and sobbed like a baby. When we were dressed, our coach had us all load up on the bus for the short trip back to the hotel. Unfortunately, it was too far to return home that night. Heck, maybe we would have all been killed by a drowsy bus driver had we gone home that night. That would have been slightly worse than what happened.

High school boys don't just do stupid things at night in a grocery store. They especially do stupid things when staying at hotels away from home after losing a game, or after winning a game, or after tying a game. Boys will be boys, and that night was no exception. So eight of our teammates decided to drown their sorrows in beer and dry their tears with cigars.

I was assigned to room with Charles, or Chuck, as we called him. Chuck was one of our linebackers, so of course he was in on buying the beers and cigars. Linebackers like to stick their heads into every play on the field and probably feel like they need to stick their head into most everything off the field as well. Chuck brought his share of the goods, or *bads* in this case, to our room. When I showed up after dinner, Chuck was already drunk on the bed.

Our room reeked of a bar, not that that's so bad, I guess. I think that some bar smells are pleasant. I've never been fond of cigarette smoke or the smell of beer. But cigar smoke? Cigars and cigar smoke will always smell good to me, because cigars mean my dad.

Cigar smoke makes me travel back in time, taking me back to fly-fishing, rides in our old '58 Buick, cross-country trips—all with Dad, our Missouri Dad. He smoked them mostly when Mom wasn't around and usually during our summer trips back to Missouri and Iowa to see Grandma, our cousins, and his old friends. Dad joked that he drove all the way back home, from Iowa to Utah, with the windows down just to air out the car so Mom wouldn't catch him.

I developed a taste for cigars during those trips. Dad once bought me a peace pipe at a tourist trap along I-80 somewhere in Wyoming or Kansas. I learned quickly that I could stick one of his cigars into the well of that pipe—and it fit perfectly. I'd puff a little of his cigar before he returned from paying the attendant for gas and buying more cigars. I don't remember ever enjoying smoking them, but I do remember enjoying looking like him when he smoked. My brothers and I even coveted cigar boxes. We regularly asked cashiers at restaurants if they had any empties, which we would turn into a treasure chest to hold our marbles, favorite rocks, and knickknacks.

That night, I don't remember Chuck offering me a cigar. I just grabbed one and lit up, without thinking, and without my peace pipe. I knew not to inhale—I suppose it's like riding a bike. When I did start thinking, however, I realized that I was doing something I shouldn't—breaking training rules, Church rules, Mom's rules. I quickly flipped the cigar out the sliding door and off the balcony.

It couldn't have been more than a few minutes later that I heard a loud rapping on the door of our room. I opened it and found a stern-looking Coach Jack Bishop looking at me. I knew immediately just by the look on his face that something was seriously wrong. He didn't wait for an invitation but strode past me toward Chuck, who was semi-conscious on the bed.

"Chuck, have you been drinking?"

"Yep."

"Have you been smoking?"

"Yep."

"Do you know what this means?" I'm not sure if Chuck, in his stuporous state, really understood the ramifications but he replied just the same, "Yep."

Coach turned and walked toward me, backing me against the wall, only stopping when his face was a couple inches from mine.

"You been drinking?"

"Nope."

"You been smoking?

"Nope."

He continued to glare at me maybe a moment too long, turned, and stormed out of the room.

A feeling of shame hit me immediately, harder than any linebacker ever had. It still hurts to some degree, forty years later. Athletes know that you just do not lie to your coach. Lie to your parents, lie to your teachers, lie to your girlfriend, your priest, but never lie to your coach.

Sure, the team was my lifeline to friends, to acceptance, to existence at my new school. But Coach Bishop was the one who welcomed me with open arms, who encouraged me, who had put me in the game. And to add insult to injury, I had lied to him when he must have been feeling as low as a coach can feel—losing a big game, finding his players drunk and puking in their rooms, and feeling a terrible remorse for not taking us home, for not watching us closer, for trusting us.

The next morning, Coach started the ride home by telling us that there would be heck to pay on Monday. Heck on Monday? Heck, I had started paying heck the night before, as soon as Coach left our room. During the bus ride home, there was no singing "99 Bottles of Beer on the Wall." No jokes. No peeing contests. Just six hours of mostly silence. I paid heck some more on Sunday, which is appropriate, since

I suppose that's what we're supposed to do on Sundays anyway—pay heck, feel guilty. It was probably the longest weekend of my life.

Monday afternoon after school, I dressed down in pads before practice and ran out on the field, only to see eight of my teammates—Chuck included—standing together off to one side in street clothes. I never dreamed that they were going to be off the team. I had imagined countless stairs, laps, gassers, push-ups. Now we realized that there would be no laps, gassers, or playing on our football team ever again. They were off the team. They were gone. And I knew that I was soon going to be gone too.

After a few remarks from Coach on training rules and the consequences of breaking them, none of which I heard very well due to the guilt, shame, and fear ringing in my ears, he excused our former teammates to leave and sent the rest of the team to the blocking sleds. The ringing in my ears gradually grew louder than the screaming in my brain to shut up and save myself. Frankly, I don't know which is worse, thinking about it years later: lying to your coach or getting kicked off the team. But I chose one. I lagged behind and walked up to our coach, like a mini death march.

"Coach, I need to talk to you," I blurted out, looking at him through wet, blurring eyes. He looked me square in my eyes, right through me, as he had done in that hotel room, and replied, "I know."

Of course he knew. As if a big, blushing, bad liar of a seventeen-year-old Mormon boy with smoky breath had not been a dead give-away? I quickly told him that I had smoked a cigar. He heard me out, laid a hand on my shoulder pads, and told me that we would talk about it after practice.

What? It was like the governor had called the prison warden to grant a stay of execution, I was that hopeful. But the executioner still awaited me.

I don't remember most of the practice but do recall that I never hit the blocking sled with more intensity. When we left the field I went straight to his office and sat down on a chair, ready for the worst. I didn't dare hope that I would be allowed to stay on the team since I had also broken training rules. I was an accomplice. Finally Coach Bishop broke the silence and the news. I would be allowed to stay on the team, in large part thanks to Chuck. My roommate, Chuck, who was now off the team, had saved me.

Coach Bishop went on to inform me that he and the other coaches had spoken with Chuck about me. He confided that Chuck had stood up for me, explaining to the coaching staff that I had not been with them when they purchased the beer and cigars, and adding that I hadn't drunk any of the beer. Chuck had actually called me a "victim of circumstances." Coach then noted that the staff had asked Chuck if they should also kick me off the team. It would have been understandable if Chuck had taken me down with the rest of the eight. He told them no.

I finished the season with the team. I made the basketball team. I tried track and field. I made friends. I played for Coach Bishop two more years at our small college when he moved up to the next level. He kept encouraging me and even lied to me one day after my college career, saying that I had a chance to play in the NFL. A lie as big as mine.

I lied a lot in the CIA, much bigger lies, like what my name was, where I worked, and what I did at night. And I was lied to quite a lot. One woman, a liar extraordinaire, lied to my colleagues and me about her ties to a terrorist group. We call those fabricators in the CIA. She took us for many thousands of dollars and countless man-hours. Eventually she even caused the expulsion of two of our officers from this particular foreign country. Another officer, one of the best and smartest, even quit the agency over its treatment of their team, stemming from this incident. All because of a fabricator—a liar—which started a sequence of events.

During a tour in Europe, I found myself sitting across the table from a Russian NOC, or Non-Official Cover. I met him during a volleyball game at the UNESCO facility. When I read the name traces provided by CIA headquarters, I learned that he had set up one of my CIA colleagues to be pitched by his KGB comrade. I was determined to return the favor.

I decided to pitch him in return, a hardball pitch, as we called them. After a few pleasantries and once our drinks arrived, I informed him that I knew he had set up one of our officers a few years prior and warned that I did not know what the host country would do to him once they found out that he had run an operation against an ally. It was an empty threat, since I did not believe the host country would do anything at all, but I tried it.

Ivan, I'll call him, looked at me with feigned surprise and denied everything. He denied that he had introduced my colleague to a KGB officer, denied that they had pitched our officer, denied that he even knew our officer. He denied and lied. I was so surprised to hear him lie so vehemently, in the middle of a drink of soda, that I laughed mid-slurp, choked, and spit Sprite in his face. We were both surprised. He picked up a napkin and began to wipe his face off as I apologized.

Surprisingly, when he was done wiping down he confessed, "Okay, you are right. I did it." He went on to explain that the KGB had forced him to introduce their officer, to "broker" an introduction and facilitate the approach and attempt to recruit my CIA colleague—which was a half-lie. He admitted his involvement, all because I spit soda in his face. I'm not going to recommend this as a standard approach to uncovering a liar. But it worked for me.

I've run into more liars. When I retired from the CIA and after I moved to a new area, members of my church congregation informed me that one of the members was a fellow retired CIA officer. I was overjoyed to hear that. Imagine, running into a colleague in my same neighborhood!

At the next church party a friend pointed him out and I walked over to introduce myself. After a few pleasantries I asked him, "So, I was told that you are retired CIA."

"Yes," he replied, "worked there many years."

"Well, I was also with the CIA, worked in the CTC for most of it."

I noticed a slight shadow of anxiety sweep over him.

"Oh, I worked in Counter Intelligence," he responded.

"Ah, you worked in the CIC?"

More anxiety. "Um, I don't think they had that office when I was there."

"Yes, I think that we did," I casually remarked.

After that, the pleasantries turned into unpleasantries. His head dropped and he began to look at his feet. He quietly replied, "I didn't really work for the CIA. I served in the military and knew some guys that were with the CIA."

Okay, I know an Englishman so I must be the king of England. I was embarrassed for him. I still cannot figure out why he would lie about something like that, nor how he was able to pull it off for many, many years. Just his luck that a real retired CIA operations officer moved to his congregation.

A week later another woman approached me at church and told me that the impostor worked for the CIA. I told her, "I don't think so." She then responded, "Yes, he did, and actually he used to work for McDonald's and is the inventor of the Egg McMuffin." Yes, she really said that. He was a CIA officer *and* McDonald's inventor.

Why do people lie? I lied to my coach to get out of trouble. In the CIA I lied a lot. The US government paid me to lie, however. I knew that I had to, to protect myself and my family and my country, but I didn't like it. I still have a strong distaste for liars, especially those who say that they are retired CIA, or former CIA, as some charlatans on the Internet claim to be. Some men lie on online dating sites to impress women. Some women lie to men to seduce them, or maybe just because they are not feeling confident about their background.

Maybe that's why I love kids. They are brutally honest, unless they have stolen chocolate from the cupboard. My three-year-old son was once watching from the backseat as a good friend, who was overweight, struggled to hook up his seatbelt. He blurted out, "You have a lot of dinners in that tummy!"

In civilian life people lie to impress, to compensate for an inferiority complex, to escape the truth, to let their wife know that she looks good in a tight dress. They are all bad reasons.

In 1984, I was on an internship through Brigham Young University (BYU) in the Washington, DC, area. One evening we attended a lecture by the renowned investigative journalist Jack Anderson. I still remember one thing that he told us, something that I have never forgotten: "The truth has a way of eventually bubbling to the surface." It's true. Liars are eventually revealed for who they are.

Some are hard to uncover, which is why we need to be careful. In 1984 I was semi-dating a young woman who had told me that she was

Venezuelan, from a wealthy oil family, drove a BMW, was enrolled at Georgetown University, and was suffering from a brain tumor. I was lucky that I was not in love with her, because I later learned that none of what she had told me was true. That was before I had dealt with "fabricators" in the CIA, those sources who either started out liars or decided that they wanted to embellish their reporting for even more money. We constantly vetted our sources until the very end when we said goo-bye, conducting ops testing to ascertain veracity of their reporting and ultimately their truthfulness.

Over the years, I became somewhat jaded, or skeptical of people. One night, in Afghanistan, we heard a helicopter make an unscheduled stop at our base. Before we could get to the LZ (landing zone) the helicopter had already come and gone. As they left, we heard them announce on the radio that they had dropped commo gear, cameras, and money—a very large amount of money, actually. All we were told was that the money, a quarter of a million dollars, had been left next to the rear end of a burned-out truck.

When we reached the truck, we found the commo gear and cameras, but no money. That was a problem. I approached four Afghan soldiers who were sitting next to a fire not far away and, using an interpreter, I asked one who I recognized if they had seen anything else by the truck, or if anyone had gone near the items.

"No, we just saw the helicopter land and leave, and we did not move," he replied.

"Well, there was also money there, and now it is gone," I accused.

"I am telling the truth. We did not take it, and we did not move from the fire," he promised.

"We will see about that. I do not believe you."

I still feel bad about that last comment. I could see his face in the firelight as I accused him, and I saw that the words had stung. In my defense, I was tired of being lied to, month after month, year after year, but I should have held my tongue until I knew the truth. When we returned to our base soon after, without the money, the radio call came: "Sorry about mix-up, we left the money at [blank] base, not yours." I got back in my truck and drove back to the LZ to find the soldier and apologize. I'm glad that I did not wait. He was dead a short time after that, with three other soldiers.

It's not an easy thing to accuse someone of lying or to catch someone in a lie. You risk starting a conflict, hurting feelings, or causing a rift in a relationship.

Here are some things to keep in mind if you suspect someone of lying:

1) Compare what they say with what others might tell you. This is called corroborating her "reporting" with what other friends might tell you.

2) Ask them the same question several times, over time (maybe a week later), to see if the story changes. Remember, it is much harder for a liar to remember details of a lie.

3) Do they repeat the question back to you or do they hesitate, stalling for time, searching for an answer?

4) Watch body language. Do they exhibit suspicious actions like looking away, touching their face or clothes, clearing their throat, or shifting their weight?

5) Do they try to flatter you to gain your trust? Or do they openly attack you, accusing you of never trusting them?

There are many techniques to detect a lie, most of which are effective but not foolproof. Even a polygraph exam, which is administered by the CIA and most other government positions, is not perfect, and some are able to defeat it. But with some practice you can learn to effectively vet people and know if they are lying by listening and observing carefully.

In the meantime, while you practice, don't lie to others, especially your coach. Don't accuse someone of lying unless you know for sure. And especially, don't believe someone who claims to be a CIA officer and inventor of the Egg McMuffin.

10: MISSION IMPROBABLE

I have no idea why I was sent to Tahiti at the tender age of nineteen. Who goes to Tahiti as a Mormon missionary? Seriously? After I opened my letter I had to look on the map to find where Tahiti was located. Most of my friends and neighbors reacted with curiosity or some form of jealous scorn, especially those who had served in places like Detroit or Boise.

No offense to missionaries who went to Boise. I did not ask to go to Tahiti, as they did not ask to go to Boise. Don't blame a girl for being beautiful. Don't blame a missionary for being sent to the South Pacific.

When I arrived I was sent to a small island named Raiatea, which is located in the Îles Sous-le-Vent, next to Bora Bora. My first companion was a young Tahitian named Teio. He was a few months shy of the end of his two years. I think that he was done with missionary work, as most are at the end of two years. They get trunky (ready to pack their bags for home), as they call it. One day we rode our bicycles to visit a family that lived quite far from our home. When we arrived we found out that the family was not home. Teio took me to a local store, a *fare Tinito* (Chinese house). As he lay out on the bench in front of the store, I asked him in my broken Tahitian, "What now?" He tilted his head up, already half asleep, and said, "Go to sleep; we will go see someone else in a few hours." I waited as he slept, looking out over the waves as they crashed on the reef about a half-mile offshore, and wondered, *What have I gotten myself into?* I had been dating the Iron County Queen and playing college football just a few months before. Now I was sitting on a bench sweating and swearing under my breath, which is bad for a missionary.

Teio taught me a lot though, before he packed his bags. One night, before going to sleep, he told me that his grandpa had instructed him how to cook a human like they did with those early white missionaries. Teio explained that they cooked the person in a sitting position, on a large fire, and waited for the victim's head to split open. I knew that they did not continue the practice for that long. But interestingly, years later I played rugby for a college team. After one game, in the other team's club (bar), a member of the other team approached our very large, menacing Polynesian teammate and tried to pick a fight. The Polynesian man walked closer, putting his scarred, scary face inches away from the other player's, and said softly, "I kill you. I eat you."

We often visited a lady with a daughter who was about our age. We helped them harvest *copra* (coconuts) from the sides of the mountains, chopping the coconuts in half with an axe, cutting the meat out, packing it in large burlap sacks, and then carrying the seventy-five pound sacks on our shoulders down to the beach. We then spread the copra out on racks to dry in the sun. It was grueling, sweaty work. Cutting rotten coconuts would often result in a shower of maggots as they split open. Walking in flip-flops down the trail and over the slippery roots of the rainforest floor was treacherous. When we reached the beach, Teio would send a young boy up a tree to pick coconuts. We chopped the tops off the fresh coconuts with a machete, gulped down the water, and then scraped the soft meat out of the shell with a thumbnail. Coconuts never tasted so good.

I was happy to perform service for the family, but I wondered why we were there so much. Surely there were other families on the island that needed help. There were other families, yes, but not all with a beautiful daughter. When Teio married the daughter a few months later, the mystery was solved.

We took our daily bath in a stream next to a Tahitian family's home. The water, which came down from the mountains, was cold, especially in the early mornings. I was shocked at how cold the water could be, and more shocked when I watched one of their boys take the intestines from a slaughtered pig and swish it in the pool of water where we bathed. A very large, greenish-brown eel emerged from under the bank, grabbed hold of the guts, and began thrashing around. The child laughed and held on until the eel wrenched it from his grip. I still bathed in the water after that, but mostly curled up in a ball, my legs held tightly together.

After a few months I received a letter from the mission president, informing me that I was being transferred a few thousand miles away to the Cook Islands, where I would have to learn a third language. I certainly did not ask for that, either.

This time I was assigned to work with a young man named Metua Ngarupe, who was from the island of Pukapuka. I love island names like Bora Bora, Pukapuka, Pago Pago, islands so beautiful that they say the name twice. Metua introduced me to the Cook Islands. He taught me about Polynesians, about how they live. In a sense, he brought me into the culture, in from the cold.

Metua and I served on the island of Rarotonga for eight months in a small village called Ngatangiia. After a while I was convinced that the mission president had forgotten about us. We were there for so long that when I was finally transferred down the road to a village called Titikaveka, one of the women, Mama To'i, informed the other "sisters" in my new village that they were not allowed to invite me to their homes, that despite the move I still belonged to her, and that she would continue to feed me.

Women in the island go by "mama": Mama To'i, Mama Rupe, Mama Aka. They are all mamas to their own children, but also to borrowed children. When a mama is not able to care for a child, or if there is a mother who needs one, a child is shared and cared for by another mother, called a *mama angai*, or "feeding mother." Many children have both their birth mother and a feeding mother. There are no orphans or homeless children. And for me, in a way, Mama To'i became my mama angai.

But even in paradise there is hunger. Hunger comes with poverty. One night we returned home to find a pane missing from a window of our small home, which was more like my garage hut, but without the carpet. It was a simple structure with a tin roof and particleboard walls. As we entered we noticed a small neighbor boy sitting at our lone table, eating tomato sauce from a bowl with a sheepish, red smile. That was his meal—ketchup. It was a pitiful sight. Rather than getting angry, we looked for more food in our pantry, which didn't have a lot, and fed him what we could find. Metua was particularly compassionate because he understood. I knew that Metua would. Often, when we were eating at the same table, he would wait until I had finished picking the meat off my fish and then ask me, "Are you finished with that?" He would then pick what little meat was left on my fish head, including the eyeballs. Metua had obviously felt hunger before.

The islanders living in Ngatangiia grew accustomed to seeing us ride by on our bicycles—and crash. We had one light between us, and rides home along the road following the beach were sometimes treacherous. One night, as we raced to arrive home before curfew, we rode too close and our bikes came together. My right leg went into his wheel and we flipped head over tails, ending in a pile in the middle of the road. As I lay there I actually saw our dinner, a can of corned beef, fly from my basket and bounce into the bushes. I grew acquainted with hunger that night.

We crashed several more times, once when we rode through a stream that had burst its banks and run across the road. My brakes were practically worthless when dry, let alone when wet. When I lost a flip-flop I tried to brake and retrieve it, without much success. Metua's brakes were no better, and he T-boned me as I was turning around. We lay on our backs in the mud in the middle of the road for a time, our white shirts no longer white. Without a word we stood up and walked to the sea wall, sat down not far from each other, and looked out over the lagoon and the ocean farther out. We knew without speaking, we had been together that long. We knew we must be bad boys for something like that to happen.

Nights brought warm, fragrant blankets of smells, soft sounds, and secret darkness. Young women who were afraid to look at us during the day would suddenly became courageous at night, calling us from the hedges as we rode past, giggling, whistling a soft "psst" similar to the "shh" of our mothers but different, somewhat whistling the sound through their teeth. Other times, the braver women would call to us, "*Eh, orometua, aere mai!*" ("Hey Elder, come here!"). It was not always easy to keep pedaling. It's not easy for young males, of any ethnicity, to ignore beautiful young women calling from the shrubs and trees along the road on a moonlit night. We could have crashed then and there, accidentally, of course, since we were not very good riders. But we did not, so maybe we were becoming less bad boys.

One night I awoke and looked over at Metua, who I thought was asleep in his bed on the other side of the room. I noticed, however, that he was sitting upright in his bed, stiff and unmoving. I followed his gaze outside to the front of our home, where a woman stood on the porch. I could see the shape of her silhouette framed by the moon, cocky, her weight on one leg, with a hand on her hip. She did not say a word, but she was looking inside, intently down at Metua in his bed. I wanted to whisper, but I simply watched. Before I could say a word, she turned, stepped off the porch, and sauntered slowly away, the most seductive walk I had ever seen. When I later shared the experience with a Rarotongan man he commented, "Polynesian women are sheep by day but tigers by night."

Polynesians are interesting people. Before arriving in the South Pacific we were told to never compliment anything in their homes: a curious piece of advice until you learn that they will give the object to you. There is not a whole lot in their homes. Most of the families that I visited were not wealthy by any means and could not afford decorations, other than an old movie poster or family photos on the walls, with strings of shell leis hanging on them. One time I forgot the advice and gave a compliment to a lady with a small brass vase on her dining table the day before I returned to America. The next day, as another missionary and I were surrounded by well-wishers bidding us farewell, I felt someone from the group reaching into my pants pocket and slipping a small, crudely wrapped package inside. As I turned to look I noticed that it was the lady who had fed us the day before. I knew instantly what she had done but as I began to argue she placed a finger on her lips and gave me a "shh."

Another "shh" from a woman. It is their language. These sounds in any language are subtle and can mean a variety of things. Men find it confusing, but it is our job to figure it out. No wonder that we often do not know whether we are coming or going.

But whether you are coming or going, it is best to not stop pedaling.

11: GET A DATE

Let's get one thing straight right away. Women are more than their bodies.

I hate to be crass right from the get-go, but after thousands of video games and movies and television programs and millions of websites around the world, all devoted to objectifying women, that *man-mind-boggling* obsession, I want to start with that premise, with that agreement.

We need to agree that women are more than that, and put that aside. Deal?

Granted, men of countless generations from the beginning of time (except Adam, who was more interested in the apple) have wrestled with the same obsession. But they also debated some grand questions as well, such as the interaction of religion with philosophy, freedom vs. slavery, the free market vs. a controlled economy. They pondered whether the world was round or flat and gazed at the planets in our solar system. These days, it seems, we are stuck gazing at body parts. Half of the world's population—the male gender—is stuck on this banal debate with our friends, in our clubs and fraternities, and in our minds.

I would love to be able to take each man by the neck, including myself—because I have been there, since the hut—and administer the "hello-hello-anybody-home" *McFly* knock on the head. Maybe some of us, at least, would answer that knock and wake up to the real debate, which is the question of our time: Will we, as men, continue to look at women in only those terms, to devalue women to that degree? Will we? Will we keep judging women on the basis of physical attributes, mere body parts? Who are we?

This question of who we are is more important than any other question in the history of the world, more important than our understanding of economics, mathematics, solar systems, anything. It is about how we treat the other half of the world's population. It is about respect.

So let's elevate the debate. Women are more than that. And so are we. And it's not just important for women. It is important for us to arrive at the real argument. Their future depends upon us arriving at the truth, mentally, as does ours. Our future depends upon us arriving at the truth.

Now, once a man understands that a woman is more than that, he needs to know how to approach her and how to treat her.

I attended countless official functions, Independence Day celebrations, garden parties, wine tastings, and other events merely to meet—or spot—sources. It was exhausting work. I spent countless hours in taxis and subway trains, looking through my pile of business cards, often realizing that the evening was a bust. No attractive targets.

It is not easy work, not all like the James Bond movies where he saunters into the room in his new tuxedo, Bond Babe on his arm, dress slit to her hip. The movies showed espionage as glamorous nightlife, expensive cars, and caviar. I hate to burst your bubble, but it's not always glamorous, and it's often a grind.

Spotting an attractive target in the world of romance can be just as frustrating and non-glamorous. Hours, days, years at nightclubs, office parties, gyms, and grocery store salad bars can often turn up nothing but salad. No attractive targets. And if you let your frustration turn to desperation, your reward could very well be a sexual harassment charge.

But spotting is a necessary part of both espionage and romance. You have to go where the ladies are. And guess what—they are doing the same thing: going where the young men are. That is the dance. It is kind of confusing, now that I look back. There is no rhyme or reason to it. Some search for women at clubs or frat parties forever, it seems, and end up meeting their spouse at the church library, which is not a bad venue. Others do as they should, linger a short time at the grocery store salad bar, and immediately meet their mate. Some might call it kismet, destiny, or divine intervention. I call it chaos.

But there are a few skills that a man can use to bring order to that chaos and raise his odds of finding a nice woman:

The bump. The bump is an essential part of an operations officer's job. It is the first step to a relationship. It is the first encounter. Some are orchestrated, maybe even literally. At one point we were trying to meet a hard-target diplomat at European station (which is what the CIA calls an office overseas). We had very scant information on the diplomat's patterns, such as gyms or restaurants he frequented, friends, stores, and so on. We knew where he worked and lived and little else. During a discussion, a fellow operations officer suggested that we drive into the back of his car at an intersection. It seemed logistically plausible, since car crashes are a daily occurrence in that country. Fortunately, we pointed out that a traffic accident is not an ideal way to meet someone, especially someone with whom you want to strike up a friendship, and the idea was dropped.

Bumping a woman can be just as risky, even perilous. She might have a boyfriend or be married. She might be fresh from a disastrous relationship. She might not be into guys at all.

First, it is easier to bump someone when they are expecting it, such as at official functions, in the case of CIA officers. Official functions are to celebrate and socialize, yes, but they are also venues to exchange business cards and to network. It is an ideal location. French Club parties are equally conducive to mingling and meeting a nice young woman. It is "*chic, et magnifique!*"

Second, do a little pre-bump prep and observation, even if for just a few minutes. Is she with someone (like her boyfriend!)? Is she talking to someone you know? Is she wearing a wedding ring?

Next, observe what she is doing or reading or with whom she is speaking. Is she browsing through books at a university bookstore, possibly looking at a book that you have read and enjoyed? If yes, bump away. "Oh, I noticed that you are reading *CIA Street Smarts for Women*!

I gave that book to my sister!" (A little shameless self-promotion, I admit!)

If she is speaking with a friend of yours, easy! Bump her by joining the conversation! Do not barge in, but join the circle, listen to the conversation, and wait for a chance to comment. When you have a chance, extend your hand and introduce yourself. That was easy.

Is she trying to find a ripe cantaloupe at the supermarket? Share your expertise! Maybe joke that you are glad to see others who share your love for cantaloupes! A sense of humor can work wonders.

Now warning, here is the perilous part. Be bold but not creepy. Do not force the issue, no matter how attractive the woman is! My most embarrassing bump occurred in a restroom of a fancy ballroom, in Paris, France. I had been trying to bump a Chinese intelligence officer who was under journalist cover, someone I had encountered several times on the party circuit. I looked for opportunities as we both mingled among the crowd. As the night wore on, my frustration did, indeed, grow to desperation. I could not bear the thought of another wasted evening and late-night taxi ride with nothing to show for it. I followed him into the restroom and struck up a conversation as we washed up. There are bumpy roads, and there are bumpy bumps. This was a bumpy bump.

Positive Mental Images. This is a principle that many operations officers in the CIA learn. You must not let alarming, disgusting, vulgar, or otherwise naughty words or phrases exit your mouth, even if you are just repeating something you heard or something that she said. For instance, if a source in the CIA were to complain to an operations officer that "this assignment you are giving me is dangerous!" his case officer must not, cannot, repeat what the source said: "No, it's not dangerous . . . You're not going to get killed," and so on. The mere repetition of that words "dangerous," "killed," or "treason" can permanently plant that word in the source's head and connect it to the case officer. It's psychology.

The same goes for a young man's conversation with a young woman he wants to date. Repeat a vulgar joke and you will take ownership of it, because it is yours from then on in her mind. Repeat a cuss word, a disgusting comment, or a graphic, violent story that you heard, and it is yours. In her mind, you will be connected to that story or that joke. Do you want her to think about zombies eating someone's brain when she thinks of you? Do you want an image of dead baby seals popping into her head next time you ask her on a date? I think not.

Rapport-building. Once you have found an entry—either a book, a cantaloupe, or anything but "Oh, would you like a paper towel?"— it's time to build some rapport, which is friendship, affinity, or a connection. It is the same "bread and butter" of building rapport in espionage, or finding a job, or making friends. Rapport is the elixir of romance; it is that moment when you smile at her, and she smiles at you, and you know that you might, just might, not trip on your way to first base.

Building rapport is as tricky as a bump, as fragile as a butterfly. Grab it by the wings and it will never fly again. You must be gentle and kind. You must instill trust in her. You must make personal connections with her based on common interests, hobbies, and backgrounds. Sometimes it is difficult to find those commonalities, since you can't just come out and ask, "What do we have in common?" That would be awkward and ineffective. Therefore, you must elicit.

Elicitation. It almost sounds illegal or like interrogation. It sounds like what an undercover cop might do with his sources or an intelligence officer might do with his assets. It is not illegal, but it is what a spy or a used car salesman or a therapist does. It is a powerful tool for many professions.

Elicitation is also effective in rapport building—more effective than using direct questions. Asking a young woman too many direct questions is actually more like an interrogation: "What is your name? Why are you here at the party? Are you with anyone? How long are you going to stay? Are you going home with anyone? What is your major? Do you have a boyfriend? What are your hobbies and interests?" No, no, no.

Elicitation is a subtle *art* of communication, the *art* of espionage, in which a person can gain information, or intelligence, from someone without turning it into an interrogation. It is avoiding direct questions; it is sharing, exchanging, and listening. Women do it naturally, second nature. It is high time that men stop questioning and interrogating, and learn how to elicit as well. Here are a few techniques:

1. Give-to-get. This can be something as simple as giving your name. "Hi, my name is Joe." You *give* your name in hopes that you will *get* hers in response. It is actually much more polite to offer your name first, rather than asking, "Hey, what is your name?" It also allows her to decide whether she wants to give her name or not. If she smiles and replies "Hi," without responding with her name, it is a definite sign that she does not yet feel comfortable introducing herself. You might try one more time, but it is not looking good.

Give-to-get also works with hobbies, interests, school classes, or a whole range of commonalities. If you are in conversation, tell her about your uncle who raises cantaloupes in Mexico, or your mom who is a nutritionist, or the fact that you are studying to be a doctor. Share something about yourself that will continue the conversation and that might spark interest from her.

2. You-me-same-same. This is an extension of give-to-get. I used this elicitation tactic extensively during my years in the CIA. It creates connections, or ties, much like those described by the fox in *The Little Prince* by Antoine de Saint-Exupéry:

> "I am looking for friends. What does that mean—tame?"
>
> "It is an act too often neglected," said the fox. "It means to establish ties."
>
> "To establish ties?"
>
> "Just that," said the fox. "To me, you are still nothing more than a little boy who is just like a hundred thousand other little boys. And I have no need of you. And you, on your part, have no need of me. To you I am nothing more than a fox like a hundred thousand other foxes. But if you tame me, then we shall need each other. To me, you will be unique in all the world. To you, I shall be unique in all the world."

You-me-same-same may help you to establish ties with a woman, to "tame" her to the point that she is no longer like a hundred thousand other women. You can find that she is unique, and she will learn that you are unique as well. It might be something as simple as learning that you are both from Arkansas or have parents from another country or wear the same shoe size. In your sharing and her responding, you might learn that you both like pepperoni pizza or baseball or the Dallas Cowboys (they will be back!). And that little shared commonality, that little spark of a shared interest, can become, someday, a flame.

Again, that little spark can be snuffed out with a careless remark, dishonesty, or a whiff of desperation. Be relaxed. And be ready to be thrown out at first base.

And think about this. What is the worst thing that can happen? She tells you she's in a relationship or married? So what! She tells you to bug off? So what! You are in the game! We all get thrown out before we make it to first base. It is to be expected, so have that expectation that you might be thrown out. Heck, she might hit you in the back of the head with a baseball as you run.

I remember my years in Europe. The traffic in many countries is unbearable. At one post a colleague told me that he was ready to shoot someone, maybe the next someone that cut him off in traffic. I'll admit, it was infuriating. But one day I thought, why not change my attitude, not for the sake of all those people who wanted to cut me off, but for my sake? Why not go to work each day and search for someone to cut me off? Why not even pick the number—I chose five—of motorists whom I must let cut me off? In fact, they would not be cutting me off any more, because I was allowing them into the flow of traffic.

It did me a world of good. I made it to work each day not wanting to shoot anyone, and back home in the evening with less stress. So have an attitude that you might be rejected. Be ready for rejection, and if it happens then just shrug your shoulders and smile. But keep going up to bat. Be bold. And do not be desperate.

But let's say she acknowledges that the book she is reading is interesting and asks you if you have read it. So you lie and reply that you love the part about . . . *no*! You don't lie! You never lie! You do not say that you have read it if you haven't. You might say that you are hoping to read it soon or that that you have heard good things about it. If you are discussing cantaloupes, you do not say that you are a farmer from

Mexico and you grow cantaloupes for a living. Instead, you mention that cantaloupes are so good for you, and that you are glad to see people eating healthy! She smiles. You smile.

Then you blurt out, "Do you come here often?"

No!!

I met my wife at the swimming pool in Kinshasa, in the Democratic Republic of the Congo in Africa. I could have never dreamt that I might meet my wife there, despite all the traveling I did. But when I saw her, I felt my heart beat out of my chest. I saw her sitting across the pool from me and thought to myself, *If I don't walk around this pool, I will never forgive myself.* A half hour later I knew with certainty that I would have visions of her in my head forever.

I finally told myself that I must be bold and ready to be thrown out of the game. Fortunately, I observed first and formulated a bump. There were young men playing volleyball next to her, purposely hitting the ball back and forth over her head, desperate to get her attention; they were using a technique similar to my "bathroom bump." When I was ready and had built up enough courage, I walked around the pool and asked her in my rudimentary French if she would like to move so they would no longer disturb her.

It fell flat. She smiled but said no thanks; she was fine. I am convinced that despite my awkwardness, she recognized that I was showing genuine concern for her well-being. I'm sure that she also knew that I was attracted to her and hitting on her, but she appreciated the fact that I was offering her assistance. At the least the annoying young men stopped throwing the ball over her head.

I do not remember the entire conversation (my wife does!), but I shared, I *gave-to-get*, and I threw in some *you-me-same-same*. I tried to build rapport; I then fanned that little spark of rapport, and built some ties. That is how you do it, like lighting a fire in a frozen tundra. It can go out at any moment. But you slowly add larger and larger sticks until you have a flicker of hope.

3. Flattery. Compliments help with creating ties, connections, or friendship. Compliments can reveal that you are observant, caring, compassionate, protective, or a whole host of qualities.

That said, compliments can also show dishonesty or manipulation. She will detect both, especially if she has read *CIA Street Smarts for Women*. If you don't mean it, don't say it. Don't drop compliments to manipulate her. If she is wearing pretty shoes, however, and you are sincere, then say that they are pretty, or that you like her beautiful dress or interesting earrings.

4. Assumption. This is as simple as it sounds. Make an assumption, rather than asking her if she plays basketball or if she is going to your same college or working at your same factory. It is making a comment based upon what you observe or hear:

"You must be a deer hunter. I see fur in the back of your truck."

"You look like you work out." (Careful!)

"I think I saw you at the last football game."

There is a simple, subtle difference between using direct questions, which can turn into interrogating, and sharing, observing, or commenting. It will help her not to feel pressured or cornered. It is much more polite and much nicer.

5. Current Events. Bringing up a world event—elections in Mexico, earthquake, or Tulip Festival—will tell her a few things: that you are well-read, that you are concerned about the world we live in, and that you are conversant. It can be something as simple as:

"Hey, did you see the news report about . . ."

"I was reading on the Internet about the situation in Europe with . . ."

"I heard my parents talking about . . ."

Not only does this show her that you are aware of important issues and that you are interested in learning, this will also help you learn more about her, about how she thinks, how she views other countries or races, and how she views the world around her. It will also help you identify commonalities and create ties.

The ask-out. When you do feel ties and feel that you have "tamed" her a bit, and you see that she is smiling and enjoying your company, it's time to make your pitch, to ask her on a date. Here's how not to do it:

"Hey, I was wondering, if you aren't doing anything this Friday, maybe we could hang out," or, "My friends and I are going to go play Zombie Crusher 5 at Charlie's place. Want to come?"

You just stepped on your spark. Your spark is out—for a few reasons.

First, never start with "I was wondering." That is the lamest of the lame comments. You are not wondering anything. You are not wondering if you want to ask her out. You are not wondering if she is doing anything. You are going to ask this woman out, so ask her: "I would love to take you out on a date Friday night."

Second, never, ever, ever ask a lady if she is "doing anything Friday night." My mother gave me the same advice years ago. No woman wants to admit that they do not have plans for the weekend. Why would they? "Oh, I have no plans. I'm just going to sit home and eat ice cream and watch TV, like usual." Now times have changed, but the feelings remain the same. This question or comment actually pins the girl in a no-win, difficult situation. She does not want to admit she has no plans, but she might want to see you. So don't say it!

Third, don't ask a girl to hang out! She does not want to hang out. She wants you to come up with an idea, with a brilliant, exciting, wonderful, romantic date! Asking her to hang out is about as exciting as a fart in a space helmet. Don't do it. Come up with a plan. It does not have to be a trip to French Riviera, but use your imagination. Ask her to help you make cupcakes or fly a kite or go sledding. Put together a puzzle. You could take her to a movie, but that is barely not lame and will not give you many opportunities to talk without enraging the people sitting around you. Have a plan. "I would love to take you bowling on Friday night. How about seven o'clock?"

Fourth, do not invite her to play video games. That is probably lamer than not having a date or plan in mind. Again, most women want to be courted, and that does not mean NBA Street Basketball court-ed. Listening to you and your buddies scream, rant, and throw Cheetos at each other will not help the flame. That flame will be snuffed out.

Fifth, do not overdo it. In the CIA, I often invited targets, or potential sources, for a pastry, juice, or coffee at a café before I would invest the time and money in someone who is an "unknown quantity." I often found out during a first encounter that the target was not an attractive target after all, and at least I did not waste a large amount of money or time. The same goes for dates. Do not invite a girl on a first date to go water-skiing at a lake or sailing or on a vacation to Cancún. Rather, invite her to go bowling or Putt-Putt golfing or to get a pastry at the school cafeteria. It will save time, your wallet, and maybe even your sanity, because you will not be forced to spend hours in a vehicle trying to think of something—anything—to talk about.

Sixth, be respectful. Do not be one of the guys that I warned her about. There are many guys who want either to hang out or to make out. Don't be either. Consent means that if she does not want to continue affection or a relationship, then she can decide that at any time. In baseball terminology, she can decide to change her mind—to withdraw consent—when a man is just getting up to bat or when he is on the way to first base, second base, or any base. Get it? Heck, she can change her mind and decide that she does not even like baseball. We all should understand that, because baseball is just not rugby.

Seventh, create a great last impression. Say good night to her after discussing unicorns or rainbows. Okay, that might be an exaggeration. But similar to the point of not repeating or saying anything disgusting or vulgar that she will connect with you, do not say anything at the end of a date that you do not want her to attach to you in her mind until you see her again, which might be in a day, in a week, or longer. You want her to have warm, pleasant thoughts of you until she sees you again. Do not let her mentally connect you with a murder, a terrorist attack, or even an economic recession. Make sure you end your date on a positive note and allow her to connect you with positive thoughts in her mind until she sees you again, which you hope is soon.

12: TOO SLOW TO LOVE

Remember when I told you to keep pedaling? Well, that is not always entirely true. There comes a time when a man needs to stop pedaling. That lady is not going to wait forever for you to make a decision.

I met my wife on the other side of the planet. It might as well have been on another planet. I did not plan to fall in love during my TDY (temporary duty) travel to Kinshasa, Zaire (now called the Democratic Republic of the Congo). But when Cupid shoots his arrow, you better be ready.

On paper, we really did not have much in common. We were from different countries and had different racial make-ups, religions, cultures, and languages. In theory, we really should not have fallen in love. But we did. And I knew after the first few dates that she was the woman for me.

But I was afraid to pull the trigger. I kept reading our relationship "on paper" where it said that we should not be together because of cultural, language, geographic, religious, and many other differences. I kept doubting. And one night, months after I returned to America, I called her to complain that the *paper* said we should not be together. I explained that we did not share anything in common, that it couldn't work out. She paused and then answered, "Well, then why do you keep calling me?"

She did not argue or beg me to reconsider. She did not plead. She just moved, like the deer in the field before the hunter can shoot. Women will do that. They will not wait all day or all year. Can you blame them? Fortunately, when she moved she stopped again and gave me another shot. We have been married for twenty-five years.

A friend of my daughter's, a wonderful, beautiful young woman, was dating a young man, Jay, who is in our church congregation. Let me tell you, he was one lucky son of a gun. Anyway, he had probably dated her for several months when, all of a sudden, she dumped him. I knew about it, of course, through my daughter, but I did not know the reason for the dumping. Being a retired CIA officer, however, I was curious. I usually cannot stand to see intelligence not being gathered.

A few weeks later, at a youth summer camp, I saw him sitting with a group of girls at a picnic table. I walked over and sat down next to him.

"So, how are things going with you and Katrina?" I asked.

"Not so good. Katrina dumped me," Jay lamented.

"Whoa, what happened?" I said, feigning ignorance.

"Well, I don't really know why," he sighed.

At that point, a young woman sitting across from him chimed in with a broad smile, "I do."

Her facial expression showed that she had a secret, one that she could not keep.

Unfortunately, Jay was too curious to salvage his self-respect and asked, "Why?" We all leaned in for the intel.

"Too slow to love," she answered with a smile. We tried not to, but the group burst out laughing. It is hardest not to laugh when we shouldn't, like at a funeral, which this was, in a way, for Jay.

Yes, Jay was guilty of not pulling the trigger, which in this case meant holding hands, putting his arm around her, maybe giving her a kiss or showing some affection. I still chuckle at her wording: too slow to love. But as I contemplate the meaning, I feel that many men are guilty of the same charge. They are just too slow.

Now, it can be just as harmful to be "too fast to love." *Too fast* brings its own consequences and harm: unwanted pregnancies, sexual harassment, or at the worst, rape. Too fast is not good either. Remember: consent, consent, consent.

In the CIA, officers are trained—actually, the concept is pounded into us—to hit "windows." Intelligence officers are drilled to stick to certain windows of time, to not be too early, to not be too late. Missing a window—being too early or too late—can be disastrous. The same goes for a relationship, especially in the beginning. Being too early or too late, too fast or too slow, can destroy what could have been a wonderful relationship.

Back to *too slow*. At the end of my career I taught espionage, or tradecraft, at "the Farm," our facility for new recruits. We taught them all about the recruitment cycle. Some were able to master the early skills with ease but were unable to "pull the trigger," to move the relationships forward and recruit. They would waste a lot of time hemming and hawing, tip-toeing around the topic: "Well, I was wondering, maybe we can forge a stronger relationship, work together, make the world a better place, help with world peace . . . blah blah blah." We instructors, playing the role of foreign diplomats, would torture them mercilessly. "I'm not really sure what are you saying, not catching your drift at all. You mean you want me to be your boyfriend?"

Men, maintain momentum. In the CIA, we figure that if a target keeps coming back, it means that they are wanting what we are selling. Eventually, we make our pitch. After all, that's why we are the Central *Intelligence* Agency, and not the Central *Rapport Building* Agency, as a colleague of mine put it. When you have rapport, move the relationship along, seal the deal, tell her how you feel. Tell her that you really like her and want to see her more often. Tell her that you love her sense of humor, her wit and her wisdom, and that you appreciate her opinions of the world. Tell her what you feel, that she is the most beautiful girl in the world! Do not be too slow to love!

13: ASSESS

There might be nothing more important in the world than learning how to judge character. Some situations are less critical, such as deciding who to take to the prom. Other situations, however, can mean the difference between a great or terrible semester at school, a wonderful or awful marriage, or even life or death.

Judging character is more of the "bread and butter" of what an operations officer does in intelligence gathering. An operations officer must first "spot" someone who has access to the information he is seeking and vulnerabilities that will make the person susceptible to manipulation. He must then "assess" her for suitability, reliability, and other qualities that a source must possess. Next comes "developing," and then "recruitment." That is the recruitment cycle. Of course, termination of the relationship often follows, either at the end of the source's usefulness, or if the case does not work out. But an ops officer must be a good judge of character at every step of that cycle.

If the operations officer judges, or assesses, correctly, he can recruit a source who will pass valuable secrets. If the operations officer judges wrong, he might end up in prison, or dead.

There is a lot that goes into judging a person's character. After all, people do not come with an owner's manual or with a sign that reads "Beware. This woman is a manipulating, lying, cruel person. Run, do not walk, to the nearest exit." There are no signs, at least not like the signs we read on the side of the road. As a matter of fact, some women are so disguised or camouflaged that it is very difficult to see who she really is. In the CIA, officers use fake mustaches, wigs, glasses, and scars to draw attention away, hide, or mask an appearance. Women can also be very adept at drawing attention, hiding, and masking.

It is not easy to see into ourselves, let alone what another person is like inside. To make matters worse, people are constantly changing, like a river that changes course over years. Even the water you see flowing by is different from one second to the next. People might not change as drastically, but they can be just as fluid. Nice people sometimes make crude or rude remarks and act like creeps, and creeps can sometimes talk nicely and act sweet.

Operations officers in the CIA vet, or examine, potential and current sources constantly, to confirm that they have not been "turned." On any given day a good source—someone who has provided mounds of crucial intelligence—might run into the wrong person or an officer from a hostile intelligence agency, maybe walking to work, and be convinced to work against the CIA. He can go from gold to a disaster overnight. That is why operations officers continually vet, test, and assess sources, every day, until the end.

So, what is a man to do? He must vet and test a roommate, prom date, or potential spouse with the same level of attention as an operations officer.

Test. This might sound manipulative, but so what? They test us for a driver's license, and we don't call the people at the DMV manipulators. We need to see people out of their comfort zone, out of their environment, off guard, off balance, off-kilter. That is the only way to truly know someone. Women, like men, are on their best behavior on a date, in church, or at a dining table. Many people can pull off a disguise or portray themselves as something they are not, under normal circumstances. So a man needs to do like Toto from the *Wizard of Oz*: pull back the curtain and see who is behind it.

How? This might not be easy with a potential roommate. But you can test him. Ask the roommate to meet you at a restaurant or fast food cafe to discuss the rental situation. Does he arrive on time? (Is he reliable?) Does he treat the waiter, staff, or cleaning crew with courtesy? Is he polite or dismissive? Does he generously offer to buy your drink or coffee? Does he eat all the nachos in the restaurant basket? See how he reacts when you spill a soda across the table and into his lap. Does he laugh it off, or is he angrier than Donald Trump? Does he help clean up?

A year or so after I graduated from college, I was living with three roommates in the Washington, DC, area. One day I walked past the open bathroom door and saw one of them standing next to the bathtub and peeing into the tub. I asked him why he was doing that. He replied, "I don't know. I've done it since I was a kid." I'm not quite sure how I could have tested him for that behavior, frankly, but I obviously missed it.

If you meet a prospective roommate at a fraternity house or club meeting, even better. Watch how he treats others. Does he constantly boast or demand attention? Is he respectful? Is he courteous to older adults or children? Take mental notes. No potential roommate is going to be perfect. However, you might save yourself the trouble of living with a guy who sleeps in every day, abandons you at parties, leaves his dirty underwear all over the room, bristles at the slightest offense, eats all of your food, or pees in the tub. I still can't get over that.

The same goes for testing a prom date or future wife.

See her at her worst. Invite her to the gym, a powder puff football game, swimming at the beach or in a leech-infested pond. See her in the mud with leeches stuck to her legs. See her with smeared makeup or none at all. Watch her reactions: patience or impatience, strength or weakness.

See how she treats others. Is she angry at the waitress for talking silly? Does she make rude comments to someone who accidentally bumps into her at a party? Does she berate the host for running out of food or drinks? Does she laugh scornfully at the professor's mistake during his lecture? Does she laugh at the young man with autism who makes awkward comments?

See how she acts around others. Does she tell the truth or does she exaggerate? Is she kind? Does she put others' needs before her own? Does she control impulses? See how she works. Invite her to a service project and watch how she handles a shovel. Maybe she is not used to it, but see how she hard she tries.

B. D. Foley

Learning to assess or judge the character of potential roommates, fellow employees, bosses, friends, teachers, or women with whom you would like to begin a relationship, or even a potential spouse, can make all the difference in the world. It can even save your life, literally or figuratively. Be especially aware of someone trying to use their authority (as a coach, teacher, or boss) to manipulate you, those who use flattery to gain your trust or threats to intimidate you. Look behind the disguise that a predator—male or female—might use to convince you to engage in inappropriate behavior or to sexually abuse you. Assess their actions and their behavior and ask yourself if a friend, or someone who genuinely loves you, would be acting like that. If you feel that you're being manipulated or that someone is targeting you, talk to someone. Confide in your parents, a counselor, or another adult you trust. Do not go it alone.

Learn to read people. Become literate in human nature. It could save your life. It might even help you find a woman who can handle a shovel.

14: PERFECTION IS THE ENEMY OF GOOD

After waiting two-and-a-half long years to marry my wife, Jacqueline, I was not in any hurry to let her go. A couple of months after our wedding, I was assigned a trip to Haiti. I asked my supervisor if I could bring her along. He seemed puzzled that I would ask to bring my wife along, but ultimately relented, "Why not?"

When I returned to our hotel one evening after work after a few weeks in the country, Jacqueline complained that this was not the nice place I had described to her. Puzzled, I told her that I had never told her it would be nice.

"Yes, you did. You told me it is beautiful, has wonderful beaches, and is a great place to live, with lots of tourists," she argued.

"No, I didn't."

"Yes, you did."

"Did not."

"Did too."

We finally tired of our immature argument, and I figured out the source of the confusion. I told her, "I lived in Tahiti, not Haiti. So sorry to have to tell you this, but we are in Haiti, not Tahiti." Two very similar names, not very similar places.

My wife was definitely not perfect in geography. In fact, she still isn't. She does not know the difference between north and south, east and west. One day I tired of her constantly getting lost and dared her to tell me which way north was. Her eyes turned a little darker, as they do when she is impatient or angry, and she replied, "Look, north is different for me than for you. If I'm facing that way, then that way is north."

Not only does she not know geography very well, but she makes lots of mistakes with languages.

And she commits gaffes with the best of them. I am not kidding. The other day she sent me to the store to pick up "some paper toilet, soap dish, and your glass eye." It used to be confusing, but now I instinctively translate her instructions back into French, then again to English, and voilà—I know that she wants toilet paper, dish soap, and a pair of eyeglasses for me.

Our children and I often laugh at her gaffes. The other night, while watching a nature series on TV, she commented that it was incredible that a "stinky ray" (stingray) could kill someone. We've heard lots of others over the years—we especially love "talkie-walkie." When she gets tired of our teasing, she tells the children that they can mock her when their French is better than her English. That could take them some time.

Her most famous gaffe was in Greece. We were invited to visit a friend's home for dinner. The Greeks are known for their hospitality, and this night was no exception. The mother of the home, Marina, had prepared a number of different dishes and done everything she could to make us feel welcome. We found ourselves on their back patio, seated around a table, probably fifteen or twenty feet long, that was covered with food.

After lots of eating and talking, Jacqueline thought that she would pay her respects to the chef, Marina. At that very moment Marina was walking around the table and asking, insisting rather, that the guests try this or have some more of that. Jacqueline began to speak and the crowd, including neighbors and friends that had been invited to "meet the Americans," grew silent with anticipation. In her very best

Greek, and in a perfect accent, Jacqueline announced, "το φαγιτο εινει ασχημο." Translation: "This food sucks."

The group grew even quieter. I was actually chatting with a man to my left when Jacqueline spoke, so I wasn't sure what I had heard. I looked over at Marina, who had stopped in her tracks with a shocked expression on her face. I turned back to her and asked, "What did you just say to Marina?" Jacqueline's permanent smile had started to wilt, but she thought that she must have just mispronounced a word, or her accent had been wrong, or that she needed to add a little emphasis. Again she repeated the phrase, again in perfect Greek, "This food really sucks."

I noticed Marina, who looked like she had been slapped a second time. She had probably spent days preparing the rabbit and chicken and lamb and you name it—it was all on that table. I remember flinching and asking Jacqueline, quietly, while shaking her by the shoulders, "What are you trying to say? Marina is big, her husband is big, and he's a cop, and her son is big, and he's a cop, and they have guns."

Jacqueline quickly whispered that she wanted to say how delicious the food was. She had merely confused two words: "νοστιμο" (pronounced "*nostimo*," meaning delicious) and "ασχημο" (pronounced "*asimo*," meaning ugly). The group roared with laughter and great relief when she tried a third time and succeeded.

Yes, Jacqueline is by no means perfect. I know that she makes plenty of mistakes in all five languages that she speaks. Yes, five.

I've made a few, in the few languages I've tried to master over the years. I called a group of Greek cops "prostitutes" for a whole year, after a Greek friend thought it might be funny to confuse me. I've made my share, but my wife is a veritable gaffe machine.

What else? Not very good at geography or directions, lots of mistakes in all those languages . . . oh yeah, she is stubborn and has a temper; she gets mad at me when I shrink her sweater in the dryer, and she makes me go to church.

You get the picture. She's not perfect. As a matter of fact, she's not even close.

Which brings me to my point. You guys out there, waiting for the perfect wife, thinking, *I know I can find the perfect wife, with a perfect body, perfect charm, perfect spirituality, perfect, perfect, perfect.* Really? Dang, even Mary Poppins was not perfect, only "practically perfect in every way." Anyway, you guys waiting for the next woman coming down the pike, down the road, from around the next corner, hoping that she will be perfect? Like you? With your perfect pecs? It might be a long wait.

One morning I asked my daughter-in-law, Alexandra, how she made it out of college single (I'm blunt like that). She looked at me with an almost sad expression and replied, "The guys all think that they are going to find someone better around the next corner." I wonder how many of her college dates regret looking around the next corner.

In fact, this pursuit of perfection might make it a very long wait if you don't knock it off. In L.V. Krause's book *Eaten Alive* she notes, "The academicians who study online dating have theorized that one of the reasons men have gotten so picky is because of the seemingly endless numbers of choices on dating websites." She continues, "Researchers have pointed out that the Internet has expanded our dating choices well beyond our processing capacity. . . . Given the endless alternatives, it's simply too easy for a man to move on."

Men actually do not do very well in situations where there are too many choices. Sometimes it's even hard to choose a box of cereal, since there are so many brands. My dad once told me when I had returned from a semester of college with another girlfriend that I was "like a dog in a field full of rabbits." We see the same situation and results with the TV show *The Bachelor*: the man is usually very confused, and does not know which way to turn, or up from down, and the women are all feeling very heartbroken. Online dating just makes it worse, providing men a dizzying number of options, faces, figures, profiles. The numbers can start to blur.

It is even part of our society of "upgrades." We upgrade cellphones, computer operating systems, and gaming systems, so why not upgrade a girlfriend, right? Wrong.

So you see, there are plenty of wonderful women out there, and a man does not have to sample every one of them or find the perfect one or wait for an upgrade. Just pick one of the imperfect ones, one you love, and put on blinders—you know, those blinders they use to keep racehorses on track—if you have to! Look for the good in her, focus on why you love her, and do not be distracted by the fact that she makes mistakes in English or isn't a perfect size two or can't cook a perfect stew, because neither can you.

Once you have found her, go ahead and marry her. Help her become your perfect wife.

15: GET GRIT

I was actually a predator of the CIA. It is not customary for operations officers to refer to themselves as predators but that is what we are. We prey on people, or targets, and then manipulate them into becoming spies. That sounds predatory to me.

In the CIA, operations officers search for targets, first of all, with access to intelligence, as I mentioned previously. The target must have intelligence that we can take in order for our government policy-makers to make correct decisions, which does not always happen. The second criteria we look for in a target, besides access, is the presence of vulnerabilities. Vulnerabilities render targets susceptible to manipulation and recruitment. Without vulnerabilities, they will not cooperate, nor commit treason, which is what they are doing (but not something we mention to them ever). Once an operations officer has identified a vulnerability in a target, he will then work to manipulate that target and recruit him.

I targeted many sources based upon many vulnerabilities. I recruited a source based upon his curiosity, another on his arrogance, several based upon greed. Late in my career, I handled a source who was recruited solely on his desire for pornography. This was before the Internet. Imagine that: he gave up everything—secrets, his country, his pride—to obtain videotapes of pornography. These emotions, or impulses, cause people to make very bad decisions. People with vulner-abilities do stupid stuff.

One of these vulnerabilities we sought was lack of impulse control. To find a target with access to his country's intelligence, possessing a vulnerability or two, with no control of his or her impulses tossed in the equation, is like finding gold.

Here is how it happens in espionage. We identify a target with little sense of impulse control feeling an impulse (greed, anger, jealousy, curiosity). An intelligence officer will reach out to the target, maybe bump him at a party. That operations officer will find out about the impulse, bring it up in a conversation, and dangle a solution in front of the target's nose. The target surrenders to the impulse (such as revenge), agrees to cooperate, and worries about the consequences later.

Here is how it happens in our world. A man who is overweight might be trying to cut calories, but he lacks impulse control. He then encounters a doughnut shop, which will reach out to him with smells and images from their store in the shopping mall. The target surrenders to the impulse (hunger), buys a dozen, and worries about the consequences later.

And it happens in relationships. A man in a committed relationship who lacks impulse control and is feeling lonely, angry, or unappreciated (any of a number of emotions), might be on a business trip and encounter another woman. He might feel that impulse (sexual) when she reaches out to him, maybe with a look, from across the restaurant. Again, he might surrender to that impulse, be unfaithful to his girlfriend or wife, and worry about the consequences later.

All these acts come about due to lack of impulse control.

Just what is an impulse? The dictionary defines it as "a sudden strong and unreflective urge or desire to act" such as to eat, drink, sleep, cheat, steal, or lie. They are all impulses, or unreflective—thoughtless—urges.

In a *New York Times* article titled "What Drives Success," Amy Chua and Jed Rubenfeld point to "impulse control" as a quality that helps individuals, and eventually a whole culture, succeed. They write,

> "It turns out that for all their diversity, the strikingly successful groups in America today share three traits that, together, propel success. The first is a

superiority complex—a deep-seated belief in their exceptionality. The second appears to be the opposite—insecurity, a feeling that you or what you've done is not good enough. The third is impulse control. . . .

"Impulse control runs against the grain of contemporary culture as well. Countless books and feel-good movies extol the virtue of living in the here and now, and people who control their impulses don't live in the moment. The dominant culture is fearful of spoiling children's happiness with excessive restraints or demands. By contrast, every one of America's most successful groups takes a very different view of childhood, inculcating habits of discipline from a very early age—or at least they did so when they were on the rise."[2]

Chua and Rubenfeld are right. Everything in our current culture seems to be screaming, "Indulge yourself! If it feels good, do it! And do it now! Buy it now! It's my money, and I want it now!" Remember that one?

Actually, that thinking has always been with us. There have always been people that told us to not wait, to not worry about it, to indulge, to not control our impulses. But it is wrong thinking and actually a sure way to weight gain, addiction, infidelity, treason, and failure.

The good news is that good boys can control bad ideas. The bad news is that it doesn't come easy. You don't wake up one morning and say, "I am going to be the master of myself today." It takes time. Lots of time. I swore that I was going to lose ten pounds before the holidays. Instead, I gained five. I swear that I will write every day, and I don't. Actually, I swear that I will no longer swear, and I still do. But I'm getting better, day by day.

Chua and Rubenfeld continue, "The way to develop this package of qualities—not that it's easy, or that everyone would want to—is through grit."

I know the definition of grit from the movie *True Grit*—both of them. The heroine in the plot, a young woman who was attempting to capture her father's killer, is the very definition of grit: relentless, determined, resolute, teeth-clenching courage. The young Mattie Ross, played by Hailee Steinfeld in the most recent adaptation, was the epitome of grit. So was Rooster Coburn. They do not rest until they find Tom Chaney, her father's killer, and kill him.

There are countless examples of real-life grit in sports, business, and academics—there are too many to mention. But to get impulse control, we need to first get grit. And I believe that we need to practice grit and impulse control like anything else. Everything takes practice.

During my years as a CIA instructor, I witnessed many examples of young recruits who showed grit in overcoming severe challenges in order to finish the training and graduate. Some could not put two words together that would make sense; others had problems of time management or lack of attention to detail. The recruits who recognized their weaknesses, however, and worked hard to correct them, usually graduated.

If you do not have an opportunity to chase after Tom Chaney, then find other ways to get grit and tame your impulses. In Edward Rice's biography of Sir Richard Francis Burton, *Captain Sir Richard Francis Burton: A Biography*, he writes that Burton used to set a bowl of sugar and cream on the table in front of him to test his willpower. Once he proved his resistance, he would eat it to reward himself! He thought of a way to get grit, but admittedly not much.

I will admit, I sometimes look for ways to practice getting grit. I practice pain, like others do, by working out in the gym, by being thirsty or hungry on a long hike, or by enduring the cold. No, I'm not a masochist; it's just part of practicing to get grit.

Some might argue that going to the gym will not help much to develop grit. I look around my gym and see ample parking outside, heating and air conditioning inside, with comfortable, padded seats, even TV screens at each station. Maybe gyms will develop a lot of muscles but little grit, maybe no more than a bowl of sugar and cream would. Maybe a better gym would be carrying logs through deep snow or sand, chopping wood, or carrying bales of hay. I'm not sure how many members would join that gym.

So what do we do if we have no chance to chase Tom Chaney or do not live on a farm in Alaska? Then we need to look for other opportunities. Start slow if you have to by just getting out of your car and riding a bike. Take the stairs rather than the elevator. Walk rather than ride. Hike rather than walk. Better yet, hike in the rain. Better yet, run in the rain. And when those impulses to stop enter your head, practice dismissing them.

Inner voice: *I'm cold*! Inner response: *Quit your whining!*

Inner voice: *I'm hungry*! Inner response: *We'll eat something later!*

Inner voice: *I want a tattoo of my girlfriend's name on my butt!* Inner response: *Dude, that won't be such a great idea when you are married to someone else.*

Inner voice: *I'm tired!* Inner response: *Do you want a promotion and that new car? Keep working!*

Inner voice: *That guy's wife is hot!* Inner response: *Okay, we looked and we looked again, now look away.*

Inner voice: *I think I'll go watch some porn.* Inner response: *How will we feel after? Let's go do something else instead.*

Inner voice: *Hey, that guy cut me off! I'm going to beat him senseless!* Inner response: *Chill! Take a breath! That's right, breathe, let it go, breathe again.*

Like I said, it's not always easy. Sometimes we even need to shout down those voices and practice getting those impulses to shut up or that anger to simmer down. But we can do it. I'm going to lose those five pounds and then five more. And then I will work on controlling those other impulses, which are many.

2. Amy Chua and Jed Rubenfeld, "What Drives Success?" *The New York Times*, Jan. 25, 2014.

16: TEA WITH KHAN

Men sometimes have impulses to kill, even when driving down the street in a civilian vehicle. According to the National Highway Traffic Safety Administration, 1,380 people were killed on highways from 2008-2016 in road rage incidents. That is a lot of people, a lot victims, a lot of needless, pointless pain for surviving family members.

During a tour to Afghanistan, my team and I were chasing a warlord, Pacha Khan Zadran, who had been firing missiles into a nearby town and sometimes at us. We planned to eliminate him and his men—most likely kill him—since he had refused to stop shelling the town. Our decision to kill him was more than an impulse, actually. He was causing us real problems, killing people and jeopardizing our mission.

One day, as we were searching for him in the area, our convoy drove right past his on a dirt road. Members of our military, CIA officers, and Afghan soldiers were armed to the teeth, as were they. Both sides were visibly startled as we passed each other on the dirt road, staring at each other through open windows. As we crossed paths, however, we noticed the taillights of their vehicles illuminate and their vehicles stopped. We stopped dead in our tracks as well, ready to fight. Suddenly, however, and to our surprise, one of the warlord's henchmen got out of one of their trucks and ran back toward us. As he approached, we sent our interpreter to find out what they wanted. After a few minutes, he returned and relayed the message. Pacha Khan had invited us to tea.

My military colleagues were as surprised as I was; we shrugged and decided to accept the invitation. We slowly turned our vehicles around and followed them to a compound, which was not far away. As we exited our vehicles, several members of our US military special forces spread out, guns to the ready. A few of us and our interpreter entered a small room of one of the rudimentary buildings inside the compound while other soldiers stood guard outside, carefully watching Pacha Khan's men. We seated ourselves on a rug on the floor, rifles by our side, and began a discussion. After some pleasantries, if they could be called that, I spoke to Pacha Khan.

"Do you know the best way to destroy your enemy?" I asked.

My interpreter, a young Afghan man, turned toward me with a worried look on his face, and said nothing. I repeated my statement and asked him to translate.

Pacha Khan's fearsome face grew even more menacing, and he did not answer.

As he glared at me, I answered my own question, "By making him your friend."

After my interpreter spoke, one side of Pacha Khan's mouth turned up slightly, probably as much of a smile as he could manage. The tension in the room slowly abated, and we talked. We drank our tea, ate biscuits, and even joked a bit. We left back to our base, no shots fired, no one dead. We did not know at the time what the results of the meeting would be, but, miraculously, he stopped shelling the town, stopped killing people, and actually joined the central government, all because we were all able to control our impulse to kill each other.

Sometimes, you can handle a situation without violence, maybe just by telling the person to stop what he is doing or saying or how he is acting. As Sun Tzu taught in *The Art of War*, "To subdue the enemy without fighting is the supreme excellence." In a way, we subdued Pacha Khan.

True, despite our best efforts to stay calm and defuse the situation, it might turn into a fight. It could even turn into a beatdown—of us. But that's okay. It might hurt and we might bleed, but it will be a good beatdown, because we stood up when we needed to. We stood up for someone else. Then again, we might stand up for women *and* give the beatdown by bouncing the bad guy's head off a wall. That might happen, and what could be better than that?

But sometimes we can control our impulse to kill and instead defuse a situation. Maybe no one died in that room because of what I said or simply because Pacha Khan didn't want to die that day. But maybe it was because we all controlled our impulses. And, if a bunch of CIA officers and soldiers, armed to the teeth, can drive by an Afghan warlord and then agree to accompany him for tea, then you can drive by someone who cuts you off in traffic or flips you the bird. You can just take a breath and control yourself. You can maybe even tell the other driver that you are sorry or that you are glad that you didn't run into each other. Heck, invite him for tea.

But do not let a simple traffic incident escalate to violence, which might change your lives forever. Let it go, let him go, and both of you go home.

17: SHAKE HANDS, FIND TEETH

Rugby can help men get grit. Okay, maybe baseball can help, too, but rugby is just . . . grittier.

I began playing the sport—the best in the world, hands down—shortly after my second knee surgery and after my surgeon and college football trainer had told me to move on from football. I imagine that he was not suggesting that I "move on" to rugby—maybe chess or music. For those of you who have seen a rugby game, you probably question the wisdom in even considering playing such a rough sport after two serious injuries to the same knee. Those of you who have played rugby will understand the attraction.

After my second knee surgery I decided to attend school in Hawaii. I was missing the islands, since I had just returned from Tahiti the year before, so it was a good fit. I enrolled, found a job at the Polynesian Cultural Center, and was settling in nicely.

It wasn't a month after I arrived, however, that I saw some of the rugby team training out on a "pitch," or rugby field. I watched for a few minutes and wondered what it would be like to play. Hey, maybe I could just join them for a run, maybe play "touch" rugby. Right. One thing led to another, and I soon found myself on a rugby team made up mostly of Tongans, a few New Zealand Maoris, and one haoli (white guy)—me.

I've heard it said that if you find yourself doing something and you are all alone, there might be a reason. If I had heard that pearl of wisdom then, I might have looked around and wondered why I was the only white guy on the pitch. At least I would have recognized what I was getting myself into. It is a downright dangerous game. It is dangerous enough when you play with other white guys. It is suicidal to play with Polynesians. It's no mystery why the NFL is made up of so many Tongans and Samoans and other Polynesians. They are big, they are tough, they are fast, and they like to fight: the essential ingredients of a good rugby player. They make the transition from rugby to football with ease, and they probably wonder why they have to wear the helmet and all that restrictive padding.

I don't think that Polynesians really need helmets. I was sitting in a Tongan language class one day when a Samoan student came in and spotted a Tongan classmate. He walked up, grabbed the Tongan by the sides of his head, and head-butted him. It sounded like two coconuts being smacked together. The impact would have knocked any normal haoli unconscious. The two of them just laughed.

They don't seem to feel cold any more than they feel pain. I went night diving with a Samoan friend, looking for octopus and fish in the lagoon off Laie, Hawaii. I was shivering after a half hour and ready to get out of the water. I saw his light moving from reef outcropping to outcropping long after I came in.

It was not just the cold that made me stop. I shot one octopus, turned his head inside out, and put him inside an old, mesh gym bag I had tied to my belt. I began swimming and searching again and shot another, slightly larger than the first. Before I could even take him off my spear, a Hawaiian sling, I saw another out of the corner of my eye. I reloaded quickly and shot the third. As I was starting to pull the third octopus off my spear, the second reached out and wrapped his eight arms around my arm. It was a creepy feeling as his suckers clamped on and would not let go. At just that instant my gym bag drifted closer to me, and eight more legs wrapped around my leg, and inner thigh.

I shot to the surface and tried not to scream. I don't know if I wet my wetsuit.

Tongans and Samoans are from neighboring islands, but they are often anything but neighborly. Think Greeks and Turks, the Hatfields and McCoys, Alec Baldwin and Kim Basinger. Many of our games with the surrounding Samoan club sides began and ended in brawls. It often got to the point that the referees just could not eject every player from both sides and figured that it was best to end the game before anyone, including themselves, died.

I felt like I was going to die during my first match. It has always been difficult to find shoes for my size 15 feet. Finding a rugby boot was even harder to find, especially back in the '80s in Hawaii. I hadn't planned on playing rugby when I went to Hawaii, so I hadn't taken any boots with me. But, hey, since I was going to be stupid enough to play rugby on a bad knee, with huge Polynesians, why not play barefoot too, and without a mouthpiece?

What I remember most of that first game was pain. It was two halves of pain. And the line-outs—which is basically a jump ball between opposing teams, both facing the sidelines—were the most painful. One opposing player facing me spotted the tall white guy and looked at me, looked down at my bare feet, looked back at me, and then smiled. I don't remember it being a warm, Polynesian *aloha* smile. I remember it being more like an *I-kill-you-I-eat-you* smile.

At the time I considered myself a good jumper. But I found that it is hard to jump with someone else's boots on top of mine. It soon became hard to run, then eventually hard to walk. I think that I spent most of the game trying to save at least a few toes.

The game went from bad to worse. I counted eleven injuries from head to toe by the end of the game: jammed fingers, cuts, hernia, missing toenails, loose teeth. The worst of my injuries was not the hernia. You can let those go for quite a while. I used to hold my breath and make it pop out so far that you could see the bulge through my rugby shorts. The worst were two top front teeth that I knocked mostly out and had to bite down on during the second half to keep them in. Root canals have kept them in since then.

It could have been worse. A couple of years later, while playing back on "the mainland," I grabbed an opposing player who was running for the try line (end zone), by his jersey. As I stopped he swung around me and met his teammate, who was following him in support. Their two heads connected and made the same sound as those two head-butting Polynesians, like two coconuts. Except these were two white guys, and it sounded more like a couple of eggs. In the blur of movement and swirling bodies I could actually make out small white particles flying through the air. The player who had been running with the ball fell lifeless to the ground.

A thought came into my mind, *Oops*. I looked down at him as he lay on the ground, facing the sky with an open, gaping mouth. Those white particles had been his teeth, upper and lower. He now looked a lot like Walter Brennan, that old actor who played the toothless cowboy cook in western movies.

I stood their for a moment with *oops* playing over and over in my mind until my teammate, a New Zealand Maori, came running by, grabbed me by the jersey, and yelled, "Come on, leave him!" You see, in rugby the play does not stop for injuries, or missing teeth, or even death, unless the ball goes out of bounds or a player commits a penalty, which does not include swinging a player around and cracking his head on another player's. I actually felt like I was in one of those World War II army movies where the platoon sergeant screams at a soldier to leave an injured comrade behind, because he is too far gone, or maybe because there is no time to save him because of the advancing enemy. The only difference was that this downed man was not pleading heroically, "Just go, leave me and save yourselves." Rugby is a lot like war, when I think about it. So we left him.

In our defense, it wasn't like we left him for a long time. When the referee blows his whistle both teams look around and see if anyone is missing. A few of us from both sides jogged back to where the player, let's call him Walter, still lay on the ground, and began sifting through the grass for his teeth. As his players lifted him up, I collected the teeth from the other players, grabbed Walter's arm, and placed them gently in the palm of his hand. He looked down with that cavernous mouth of his and gave a little moan. In hindsight maybe I should have given his teeth to a teammate, who could then have washed them, put them in a sandwich bag, and presented them to him in a more appropriate setting, like a dentist's office.

I eventually had my own teeth fixed when I returned to the mainland. I complained to the dentist, a girlfriend's father, that my two teeth hurt when I tapped on them. He looked at me with a quizzical expression on his face and suggested, "Then don't tap on them." I think that he must have been relieved when his daughter and I broke up.

Many of the Polynesian rugby players have almost a Dr. Jekyll and Mr. Hyde personality. I remember playing in one rugby match against Arizona State. During one play I had a "misunderstanding" with an opposing player. I felt like he should have released his grip on my jersey immediately after tackling me. He felt like he needed to hold on longer, to stop me from rejoining the flow of the ball. So I settled the disagreement by punching him in the face.

A few minutes later our two teams were pushing in a "scrum." I love rugby terms like "scrum," "maul," or "ruck." Even the words sound rough and manly. You won't hear about a ruck in synchronized swimming. Or tennis. Forty-love? Give me a break. Coaches regularly scream, "Ruck him out of there," which basically means to give an opposing player "the boot."

During the scrum we tried to push them over the ball so our "scrum-half" could grab it and pass it back to our "backs." The other team tried to push us backwards. As I pushed I felt my fellow "second row" teammate's arm go back and then quickly forward with a thud. It sounded a little like the guy's head hitting the wall in that Paris subway. Anyway, he had punched the opposing side's "hooker" (there's another term you won't see in synchronized swimming) in the face. As the scrum broke up and players ran after the ball, the Arizona player was left lying on the ground holding his face. I ran alongside my teammate, a huge Tongan with fists the size of hams, and I asked, "Why did you do that?" not in an accusatory way, just curious. This huge Polynesian looked at me quizzically and replied, "Brah, you started it."

That was all it took to switch Dr. Aloha to Mr. Hide—hide yourself, hide your wife, hide your kids, hide everyone. When he had seen me punch one of the opposing players he knew that "it" had started.

"It" was on. Paula—yes, that was his name, pronounced Pa-oo-la (*you tell him it's a girl's name*)—was no longer the fun-loving, laid-back, aloha guy. He was Dr. Dangerous. I suppose that even us white players get a little that way. But I do not think that Paula ever thinks *oops* after he punches someone.

I have no regrets that I took up rugby after tearing up my knee, despite undergoing a third operation when my rugby days were over. I think that it toughened me up. How could it not? Rugby is a man's sport. Actually, it is a tough man's sport. Seriously, it is a tough, crazy man's sport.

Rugby has changed me in many ways. My knees ache in the winter, and I can't walk up stairs very well. My shoulders hurt a lot in the morning. But also, it has changed me on the inside. I don't think *oops* anymore. I believe in playing hard and shaking hands at the end of the game. More importantly I believe in helping find everyone's teeth.

18: DJIBOUTI DUTY

He wasn't the first terrorist I had ever met. I had been introduced to another from a different terrorist group a few years earlier, one who had been cooperating with a European service and was offered to us to debrief. That time we had spoken in a fancy European office, everyone dressed up in suits, all sanitized and civilized.

My second encounter with a terrorist was not like that. I had traveled to Djibouti, Africa, to meet him in a prison. No nice office, no tea.

My interviewee, let's call him Ahmed, had confessed to a bombing and was serving a life sentence. When I arrived I noticed that there were very few guards and very little security. I actually wondered why the prisoners did not start an uprising and crash the gate. Maybe life was better for them in prison. When I served in Afghanistan, we captured a man for supplying weapons to the Taliban. After a few months of detention, we decided to release him. The only problem: our prisoner did not want to go back to his home or family. He was enjoying the food and treatment too much. After more arguments to convince him, I finally told our Afghan military officers to take him to town and buy him an ice cream for his journey home to lessen the blow.

A prison is not the safest place to interview a prisoner. In 2001, a CIA officer, Mike Spann, was gathering information from Taliban prisoners—including John Walker Lindh, the American who was aiding the Taliban in Afghanistan—when they rioted and overran security. Spann, a wonderful young man with a new family, was brutally killed during the uprising. He was the first American to die during the Afghanistan war. At that point in my career, I was used to harsh places and harsh conditions and knew that I had a job to do, so I went ahead with the interview.

I first met the prison warden, a rotund, well-fed man who looked a lot like an African Buddha. He spoke excellent French and was courteous and jovial. He told me that Ahmed was fitting in well with the other prisoners and was not causing any trouble at all.

Ahmed was soon escorted into the room and sat down across from me. It's not easy to make nice with a terrorist who has killed and injured so many people, but I figured that I would first try to establish some rapport. I began by asking him about his past few years in prison. Ahmed replied that he was first tortured by the government officials. I looked over at the African Buddha, who smiled and nodded his head.

"I was placed in a metal box and did not see the sun or moon for several years."

Buddha nodded his head in the affirmative.

"I was beaten, but carefully, so there would be no marks on my body and the French magistrate would not know about the torture."

Buddha nod.

"Other times, they sat me back in a chair, tied me up, and drowned me with water [waterboarding]."

Buddha nod.

When Ahmed was done venting, I asked him about his involvement in other terrorist attacks in Europe. He was not about to confess to anything else, obviously. He obviously did not want to go back into the box or be drowned again. He stuck with his story, that this was the only time he had ever participated in terrorism, and that he was done with that part of his life. Maybe so.

I returned to Europe and never heard of him again. I wondered if he had ever been let out of prison. Then I thought, why not check to see if he is on Facebook? I found him, smiling in a family photo, living in Europe. I don't know that I will send him a friend request.

19: USE THE TRUCK

Our youngest son did not come easily into this world. My wife, Jacqueline, and I had tried for years and years for another child, with no luck— even after taking her temperature, avoiding hot tubs, and having her stand on her head, which was one piece of advice from a friend. We finally gave up on having any more kids right before my departure to Afghanistan. I don't know what happened during my tour—maybe being around all those big guns increases testosterone levels? Whatever the reason, when I returned home my wife became pregnant and nine months later our third child appeared.

Brandon was born tough or with a guardian angel, or both. When he was one month old my daughter, Shana, dropped him when she tripped over the dishwasher door that had been left open—he landed on his head on the tiled floor. A visit to the ER ensured that he was okay.

The very next day I was babysitting him at home while Jacqueline went to do errands. I decided to take him for a ride in his stroller, as any dutiful father would do. I carefully wrapped him up in blankets and strapped him into his stroller. But as I was pushing him down the driveway, I remembered that I hadn't locked the doors. What to do now? Should I unload, unstrap, unwrap, and remove him from the stroller? Or just quickly run in and lock the doors? I chose the latter. When I came back outside he was gone. I frantically scanned the garage—nothing. I looked outside—nothing. My eyes followed the driveway, and I saw the stroller in the road, upside down, the wheels spinning. I ran as fast as I could, lifted the stroller, and saw him, still strapped in, his face as red as a beet, hands clenched by the sides of his face. I waited for some sign that he was okay, but nothing. He finally let out a scream. A scuff on his head was the only sign that he had been in an accident. I was scared to show him to my wife, so I took him to a friend's wife and handed him over, saying, "Here, take him. He's safer with you."

A few years later he was learning to read. I learned how to cut out, glue, and color with crayons during my kindergarten year. The over-achiever parents have obviously won the debate on when kids should learn to read. One night I was congratulating him on how well he was reading a Dr. Seuss book, *Hop on Pop*. "Yep," he responded, "I can even read with my eyes closed." And he closed his eyes. When he noticed that he couldn't see the words, he squinted from one eye and continued reading. "Nice," I told him.

He is our party animal and is totally aware of all things "party"— holidays, birthdays, treat days. He has calendars where he crosses off days. He constantly asks, with his fingers up in front our faces, how many days before such-and-such party, campout, or whatever. He advised us on Christmas Day, "Easter is next." But for a party animal he also has quite the killer instinct.

While living in southern Virginia, I grew obsessed with hunting whitetail deer. I was often so eager to hunt that I would forget to eat dinner—and I never forget to eat.

The deer in that area are rather small so it took a few to fill a freezer. I shot six in 2006 and four more in 2007. The locals taught me to dress and butcher the venison. I grew comfortable cutting up the steaks and roasts, and my family grew really fond of eating them. My wife actually came up with an incredible recipe of beef bourguignon using chunks of venison instead of beef. Wow.

Brandon, who was four years old at that time, came to the hunt shack most times that I shot a deer and watched as I dressed it and later cut up the venison. I was glad that he and his older sister and brother had the opportunity to learn firsthand about hunting and cleaning game. He grew comfortable with the whole process—from sitting in a deer stand to seeing dead deer in the back of my truck to packaging the steaks. In hindsight, however, I would say Brandon's perception of deer "devolved." In his mind, he visualized all deer hanging upside down, steaks on hooks, rather than as Bambi prancing in the meadow with Thumper.

I realized just how aggressive his attitude had become with regards to deer after my second year hunting. We were driving home one evening past a large field when I heard a husky voice from the backseat of my truck, "Kill, Papa . . . kill, Papa." For those writers that think a comma does not make a difference, those two commas are crucial. At the time it sounded a lot like "Kill Papa, kill Papa." The hair on the back of my neck actually stood on end, but I managed to respond, in a nervous voice, "Brandon, is that you?" He replied, "Kill the deer, Papa, kill the deer—eat the deer."

Brandon had seen a herd of deer emerging from the trees to graze in the field. Or rather, my little Neanderthal had seen a whole herd of packaged venison steaks, ready for shooting, cutting up, and cooking. Amazingly his already husky voice had instinctively morphed into that low raspy voice you hear on cable TV hunting programs, when the guide whispers in the shooter's ear, "Now, take him, now!"

During the next few weeks, my friends and I had plenty of laughs about his "caveman" comment to kill and eat the deer. Some of my wife's nature-lover friends cautioned that we should not expose Brandon to so many dead animals at such a young age—that maybe we could feed him more salads, take him to a zoo or two, or rent the *Bambi* video. We laughed at that suggestion.

About two months later, however, Brandon and I were driving home through the same area, again around dusk, and saw another group of deer not far from the road. Brandon spotted them instantly and again shifted to his hunter voice. "Kill the deer, Papa," he whispered. I was more amused than alarmed this time. I jokingly informed him that I did not have my gun. He whispered back, again in his hushed hunter voice, deadly serious, "Use the truck."

20: USE THE BIKE

It was tempting, but I didn't use the truck on those deer. That would be silly, as silly as using a bicycle.

I once used a bicycle, however, during the summer of 1997.

My family and I were visiting my parents, on home leave prior to our posting to overseas. We had just finished a tour in Europe, where we loved our European friends but hated the congested traffic. And that traffic got me thinking—maybe I ought to commute by bicycle during my next tour. And why not get a rugged mountain bike to ride in Utah and then navigate the cobbled streets of another congested European city?

There is a bike shop about two blocks from our family home. Brian, the owner, helped me pick out just the bike for my six-foot-five frame: an extra large, super rugged, Wahoo brand. It arrived a week later and I was soon ready for my first ride. One side note—Brian also tried to sell me a bike helmet—but I didn't want one. Heck no, and I told him so. "Never needed one in forty-something years—helmets are for sissies."

Kirk was a mountain biking fool in those days. I've known Kirk ever since I was around eight years old. He grew up down the street from our home, and I spent most every day of my childhood summers jumping on his trampoline, riding his mini-bikes and motorcycles, and climbing his trees—usually to spy on his much-too-shapely-for-a-six-teen-year-old sister, Julie. Like many teenage girls, Julie liked to suntan in her backyard, and the trees offered an excellent vantage point. Let's just say that Kirk's backyard was a boy's Shangri-la. And do you want to hear something funny? Kirk still thinks that all the neighborhood boys were at his house every day just to see him.

Back to that fateful summer day, early afternoon. Kirk suggested that we try out my new bike on the "C" trail. It is a tradition in most Utah towns to have an initial for the local high school or college branded on a nearby mountain. The "C" is a huge, whitewashed letter located a few thousand feet up the side of the mountain. It is accessible by a dirt trail up the face or by Right-Hand Canyon Road, a winding, paved road to the backside of the "C."

The view of the entire valley below makes it worth the ride, but the trail is not for the faint of heart—which I am not—nor the beginner—which I was. It is very steep and rocky, and includes plenty of challenges: juniper trees, gullies galore, and sharp switchbacks. Fanatic mountain bikers like Brian pride themselves in riding to the top without stopping.

As I hopped off my front porch and onto my Wahoo, my mom called out, "Where is your helmet?"

"Don't have one, don't need one. Helmets are for wussies. It's too hot anyway, gotta go," I called back as I road up the street. She was not happy with the answer but decided against chasing me up the street.

"Your mom is right, you know," Kirk said as we rode off.

We turned the corner and pedaled south past the mayor, out mowing his lawn. "Where is your helmet?" he called out to me as I rode past. You can already guess what I yelled back—"Don't need one, never needed one, too hot, helmets are for wimps." I was starting to get tired of people nagging me about wearing a helmet. What were we up to now? Four people had tried to get the idea of a helmet through my thick skull and convince me that my skull was not so thick that I did not need a helmet.

We then stopped by Kirk's mother's home, located at the foot of the mountain, to fill our water bottles. Kirk's mother, Carol Ann, herself an avid biker, joined our conversation in her kitchen and began giving us motherly advice. "Drink plenty of water, don't talk to strangers, wear clean underwear," all of which I ignored as usual. As a kid it was "don't track mud in my house," and more often "get down from that tree"—I'm just saying, you should have seen Kirk's sister.

Okay, where was I? Carol Ann's motherly advice included putting on a helmet.

"I don't have one," I mumbled and started to walk past her.

"You have to wear a helmet," she said and edged forward.

"Nope, too hot," I replied.

"Not too hot to crack your head open," she shot back.

"I never had one before, and I have never cracked my head open," I retorted.

She had had enough. Stepping in the doorway to block my exit, she announced with a threatening tone, "You are not leaving this house without a helmet." I knew then that I had no choice. She grabbed her husband Dave's helmet, helped me adjust it to fit, and allowed us to continue on our way.

The ride up was uneventful but difficult. It took several hours—full of my grumbling about the steep incline, the heat, that lousy helmet, and Kirk's mean mom. We arrived at the top with the sun going down and the day turning to dusk. As we rested at the top, Kirk informed me casually that on the way down we would need to brake a lot, especially around the switchback turns. "It's easy. Just lock up the back wheel so you can slide around the corners and not plunge off the edge," he advised.

What's that? Do what? I did not like the idea of going back down that narrow trail in the failing light. I did not know how to lock up the back wheel and slide around switchbacks, and this didn't seem like a good time to learn. And I especially did not like the sound of "plunging" off the edge of anywhere if I did it wrong. Is that where the name "Wahoo" came from? Wahooooooooooooooo!

We spent the next ten or fifteen minutes arguing about which route to take home: whether to return via the C trail or take the paved road down Right-Hand Canyon to the highway, then on to town. Right-Hand Canyon Road is smooth—no rocks, no switchbacks. Kirk did not like the idea of sharing Right-Hand with crazy old sheep ranchers in a hurry to get home to supper, or with young, passionate couples returning from the "submarine races" above the C. I couldn't stop thinking of that word "plunge," however, and grew more persuasive by the minute. Unfortunately, as it turned out, I won the argument.

The first part of the eight- to ten-degree descent was exhilarating, especially after laboring uphill for so long. The mountain wind quickly cooled us off as we raced, brakes off—around forty-five mph—down the mountain. I noticed immediately that it would be hard to control our speed, but I had a new Wahoo with new brakes. As I raced ahead of Kirk, who was following about fifty yards behind me, I pointed out deer grazing on the uphill side of the road. It was a fabulous, high-speed tour of the mountain for a speed demon like me—trees rushing by, deer, speed, deer, more speed, more deer. Can you see where I'm going with this?

I took another corner at breakneck speed and, heading down a long straightaway, saw a large mule deer buck spring up on the down-hill side of the road. At first he appeared to be looking away from us. I still remember thinking at the time, *I better point him out to Kirk— well, maybe that's not necessary since he's right there on the road.* I also remember admiring, while I was not braking, the antlers on the deer.

The buck, at least a four-point (that is eight antler tines for eastern-ers who count both sides), eventually heard and saw us barreling down the road and jumped into my path. Funny how time really does slow down. I remember everything in vivid detail. As the buck—let's call him Fred—and I merged, I thought, *I'll make it past him—just gotta go faster. If I go a little faster I can make it past him.* You have to understand that I am one of those people that figures I can drive faster in a rain or snowstorm, thereby arriving at my destination before any accident can occur. Think about it.

I'm no mind reader, especially with deer, but Fred must have been thinking the same thing—*I'll run faster, faster. I can make it. I can make it.* Of course, he might also have been thinking, *Brake, brake. Why doesn't this idiot brake?!* Fred made one last-ditch effort to veer away from me, to no avail. I never did touch my new brakes, but I oddly remember dragging my feet at the last second. Old habits die hard. It had worked while riding my old Schwinn ten-speed with no brakes at five mph, heading to the corner market. Foot-dragging doesn't work at high speeds. I hit Fred broadside.

The rest was a slow-motion blur. I remember flying over Fred. I remember landing headfirst on the pavement, then rolling, bouncing, and sliding for a long time. I actually remember a thought entering my head as it bounced along the pavement: *There is no way my head will be able to take this kind of punishment—I am not going to survive this one.*

When I stopped rolling I found myself flat on my back, looking up at the sky from the ditch on the side of the road. Kirk, who had seen the whole thing in real time, rode up to the crash site and stopped his bike next to me. Kirk—my lifelong friend, my companion in countless escapades, the one guy who I know has my back—gazed down at my bleeding body and exclaimed in a disappointed voice, "Dang, I wish I had that on video!"

His comment did make me smile through the pain. I slowly began to move my neck and trunk and legs, and thankfully realized that I was going to be all right. Then it hit me that I was alive because I had been wearing a helmet—the first time I had ever worn one. I slowly sat up and then made it to my feet.

. D. Foley

I was bloodied and covered from head to toe with road rash and bruises, but I was okay. Kirk was relieved to learn that the liquid he had seen spraying from my bouncing body was merely water exploding from water bottles in my backpack and not brain matter. Not two minutes after my fall, a young couple drove up in their truck and slowed down to see if we needed help. I was soon in their cab, with Kirk and the bikes in the back, and on my way home. The couple offered to take me to the hospital, but I declined.

After photos in the front yard, I walked inside. My wife, Jacqueline, and my mom saw me at the same time and looked more angry than worried. Moms and wives eventually replace "Are you okay, honey?" with "What have you done to yourself this time, you clumsy, accident-prone oaf?" when they see their more active boys after an accident. I gave them the short version and hopped in the shower to remove gravel while my dad drove to the store to buy large gauze bandages.

Mom and Jacqueline then had me lie on the floor while they bandaged the pancake-sized scrapes on my front, and then turned me over and treated my backside. Incredibly, other than a sore neck and road rash, I suffered no serious injuries. All I have to show for it now, years later, are more scars in my collection.

The helmet saved me. Actually, Carol Ann had saved me by insisting I wear the helmet. The Bell helmet was totally destroyed—cracked in half, extra bump in the back crushed flat, completely covered in deep scratches. Interestingly, I found two deep punctures in the left side—maybe from the deer's antlers. The helmet had definitely done its job.

Two days after the accident, I bought roses and a thank-you card and presented them to Carol Ann. I thank God for Carol Ann and the four other angels who tried to put some sense in my head, or save it, actually. The bicycle helmet served as a reminder to me and other riders for some years after that; Brian hung it on the wall of his bike shop with a plaque that read, "Saved by the Bell."

Women routinely ask me if the deer was okay. Kirk told me that Fred got up and ran into the woods while I was still lying in the ditch. I like to think that Fred's head is now mounted on some hunter's wall.

I was lucky that I still have my head. I hope you keep yours too.

21: TIME TO GO

I wonder if we show up in heaven—if there is such a place, and I hope there is—in such a state of dizziness from this earthly spin that we have to rest in the Arrivals Lounge. Maybe we are allowed some time—if there is such a thing—to take a break on a heavenly Lazy Boy where we hold our head in our hands, waiting for the nausea to pass. Maybe, as we sit there vomiting in a heavenly bucket, we think, "Well, that was weird."

And it goes by fast. One day I'm a bad boy of ten years, eating Cracker Jacks and watching *Jason and the Argonauts*, a movie about the Greek hero in search of the golden fleece. After the movie I can't sleep, tormented by nightmares of Jason fighting skeletons which have sprouted from the Hydra's teeth, summoned by the evil king of Colchis, or maybe by visions of Medea, the beautiful high priestess of the goddess Hecate. And the next day, it seems, I'm thirty-five years old, married to my own Medea, walking where Jason walked, and battling cars sprouting from terrifying traffic.

Some call Greece the birthplace of logic; others add that it's maybe also the death of it. Not just because of the traffic. Greeks have a different way of looking at things.

During many of our visits to Athens, Jacqueline and I often took our small son, Nolan, to parks on the outskirts of Athens. Nolan would play for hours on the playground equipment, and it was often difficult to coax him down from the monkey bars once he was up there. One afternoon Jacqueline called to him several times to climb down from one of the contraptions and ended up scolding him for not obeying.

A Greek lady, who was minding her own children but listening to Jacqueline, approached and cautioned, calmly, that "a mother should never say no to her son because it will cause him to be impotent later in life."

I am trying to remember how often my mother told me "no." I know it was a lot, several times a day. Whatever the case, I will certainly blame my mother for any problems I encounter.

I heard a story of an American man working in Greece who was involved in a traffic accident, as almost all drivers in Greece will be. He told me that as he was driving over a hill, a car approached in his lane and hit him head-on. When the police arrived, the man pointed out the location of the two vehicles, which had come to rest in his lane, and explained that he had been driving in his lane, as required even by Greek law, and that the other driver was obviously at fault. To his amazement the other driver quickly explained that it was the American's fault, as he would not have had an accident "if the American had not been there." True enough—there would not have been accident if that dang American had just remained in America.

I've never hesitated to tell Nolan "no," and we have had our share of quarrels, as most fathers and sons have. Our first fight occurred when Nolan was only a year old. I was trying to change his diaper and he began to squirm and twist, making it nearly impossible to complete the task. I stood over him, shook my finger, and told him to stop. I suppose he had heard too many "no's" because he swung his fist, the one holding his cast-iron Big Bird figurine, nailing me in the side of the head. Big Bird's beak pierced the skin and made a nasty cut on the side of my eye. Blood began running down the side of my face. I must have tried to count to ten but only made it to about three. I picked him up, carried him over to his crib, and dropped him on his butt. Of course, when he landed on the mattress he bit his tongue, which started to bleed.

My wife entered the room at that exact moment, seeing us both bleeding like a couple of heavyweight fighters. She screamed, "What are you doing to each other?" I guess that first fight would be described as a draw.

Greeks are big into warding off evil spirits. Fishermen spit on their nets. Old women spit on children. Many women spit on Nolan when we were walking around on a visit to Athens. They didn't actually spit saliva, but would make a small "pftew" sound and gesture, as if they were spitting on him. The "phtew" was similar but slightly different than the "shhh" sound my mom would make to stop me from asking more questions, and the "pssst" of the island girls to make us stop pedaling our bikes.

Interestingly, I think that the spitting worked. We never experienced any troubles with evil spirits on any of our trips to Greece.

Another interesting aspect of Greek life and culture is their strong belief that when it's your "time to go," or die, you go. I witnessed this firsthand when I was visiting a friend, Vangellis, who worked at a music store on a busy boulevard of Athens. As we talked outside his store, we saw an older man fall backward onto the sidewalk. We ran over to him and knelt down. He was unconscious and did not appear to be breathing. We loosened his necktie and collar and gently slapped his cheeks to revive him, all to no avail. A crowd soon gathered and one of the spectators approached, identifying himself as a Greek doctor. He took out a stethoscope, checked for a heartbeat, and began chest compressions. I told Vangellis that I would try and find a taxi, or better yet, an ambulance, to take him to the hospital. I waited by the side of the boulevard for a few minutes, waving my arms and calling, waiting, and hoping. But as I glanced back, I noticed that the doctor had already stopped the compressions and was standing next to the victim.

I ran back over and asked why he had stopped. He replied that the man was dead. I asked him if we could not try some more to revive him. The doctor replied again, "He is dead. It was his time." At most he had worked on the victim for two or three minutes. In his mind, it was the victim's "time to go."

I am a believer that sometimes we think it might be someone's "time to go" and we are mistaken. Maybe it was not yet his time. I ran back over to the side of the road and, as luck would have it, saw an ambulance approaching. I ran out into the road, dodging cars, and flagged down the ambulance, which weaved to the side of the road and parked at the curb next to us. The two attendants came over to the victim and began to ask questions. I interrupted that maybe they could load the victim in their vehicle, take him to a hospital (which, as I later learned, was about four blocks away), and then ask questions. The doctor turned to them and announced to the crowd, again, that the victim was dead. "Is not!" I interjected. "Is too!" he shot back. Is too, is not, is too, is not. No point in arguing any further. The doctor had spoken. ·

At that the two attendants turned and began walking back to their ambulance. I followed and stopped them, asking why they were not taking the dying victim. "We are not allowed to transport dead people," was their reply. More arguing, pleading, persuading, and they finally took him. But it was too late. I heard later from my friend that the man had indeed died.

Who knows, maybe he would have died anyway, but maybe not. Maybe it was not his time and we let him go too early.

22: NOT TIME TO GO

Sometimes it is our time to go but we are lucky. I've been lucky.

While serving in Afghanistan in 2001, I was serving at a forward-operating base. We were mainly engaged in running operations against Al Qaeda and the Taliban, with a few other terrorist groups thrown in.

We often relied on sources to bring "intel" from the surrounding villages regarding where the bad guys were hiding out, where they were looking to attack, and where they had stashed their weapons. The sources learned quickly that the more intel they brought to us, the more money they earned. Lots of money. Actually, they could make more money from one report than they could earn in a year of hard work. It didn't take long for them to figure out that they could make as much money off false reports as they did with accurate ones.

One particularly annoying source kept appearing at our base with reports of groups of Al-Qaeda terrorist camps or huge weapons caches in the surrounding mountains. When the intel proved false, he regularly explained that we had obviously not arrived at the location in time, that the Taliban had already departed, or that we had gone to the wrong location. Looking back, he was actually a very good liar. But after several meetings and faulty reporting I told him to never come back. In fact, I informed him, through our interpreter, that if he did show up again at our base, I would throw him in prison.

After a few months, our interpreter informed me that our fabricator had returned. I was surprised and a bit angry. I went to the tent and started to scold him, "I warned you and now you are in trouble." Our fabricator hurriedly claimed that he had found a weapons cache, and that this time he was telling the truth. I watched his eyes as he spoke, and he appeared genuine. I decided to take one more chance on him.

A weapons cache in Afghanistan.

We loaded our trucks and headed out in a convoy, spread out along the road so that one land mine would not kill us all. My sixth-grade teacher, Mr. Magnum, used to yell at us all during recess, lining up to come back inside, "Spread out, a hand grenade will kill you all!" This is great advice, but probably words that are no longer shouted at kids on a school playground. We eventually arrived at a small village at the foot of a mountain. We drove between the small homes, wary of an ambush as always, and slowly made our way up the mountain. We arrived at the top, and our fabricator pointed out the trench and entrance excavated into the peak. When we entered the cave we saw mounds of mortars, artillery shells, and various munitions piled half-way to the ceiling. Our fabricator had actually told the truth, for once.

The explosion as we destroyed a weapons cache.

After destroying the cache with explosive charges and collapsing the top half of the mountain, we loaded up and headed back to our base. On the way, our fabricator-turned-reliable source commented, "I know of one more cache." We drove a few more miles and entered another, smaller village. The source pointed toward a shack near the outskirts and said, "There." Again, our National Guardsmen secured the area, set up a perimeter, and entered the shack. After a few minutes, I followed them inside. Again, the cache was piled high with the same types of military munitions, mostly Chinese-made mortars and rockets.

Curious, I approached a pile of mortars on a table, and a small green box, which seemed out of place and looked more like a small child's toy, caught my eye. I walked over to it and picked it up. I immediately knew that I had made a mistake, especially as one of my National Guard colleagues hissed and went completely quiet. I had picked up an anti-personnel mine. I froze in place, holding it out in front of me, not moving. I slowly placed it back on the pile and walked out of the room, embarrassed but relieved that I had not killed us all. It was not our time to go.

I was lucky that time. I was lucky another time when I slapped a donkey in the butt as I drove past in a Humvee. I decided to never do it again when I later read a report that the Taliban had begun implanting bombs inside donkeys. Talk about an IED (Improvised Explosive Devise).

Terrorists regularly fired rockets at our base, using two nearby hills as "sights" of a gun to align the rockets. One morning a farmer got word to us that he had found a series of rockets lying in his field, having failed to launch. We soon arrived at his farm, about four kilometers from our base. Our special forces officers rendered the rockets safe, and we climbed into our vehicles, each of us with a rocket between our legs. It was a very bumpy road back to base, to say the least. We tried to talk about anything but what would happen if the road was too bumpy. One of the National Guardsmen, Justin, assured us, "Don't worry about it. If anything happens, you will never know it."

Others were not so lucky. At a nearby base a group of my colleagues had retrieved a cache of Chinese-made weapons, similar to the ones we found, which included hand grenades. The Chinese writing on the box prevented them from deciphering what kind of grenades were inside. But they foolishly decided to have some fun and take the grenades to their base range to throw. That's what guys do. Guys like to blow stuff up, remember? Two of them climbed into a trench. One of them grabbed a grenade, pulled the pin, and tried to throw it down range. The grenade detonated next to his head, immediately after leaving his hand, killing him instantly. Shrapnel also ripped through his friend, who was lucky to only lose his hand. From what we heard at the time, it was either a defective grenade or it was not meant to be thrown, since there was no delay built into the firing mechanism.

Others are lucky, and it is not quite their time to go. Another colleague in the CIA, a close friend, Kent, was traveling through the desert in Iraq during the first Iraq War. As he and his colleagues were driving, they noticed an exposed land mine lying around fifty meters off the road. They stopped their vehicle and all thought, probably in unison, *Wouldn't it be fun to shoot at it with our Browning 9-mm. high-power semi-automatic pistols?* Boys will be boys, no matter the age. *Let's blow stuff up!*

They each began to take turns shooting at the mine, which was a powerful anti-tank mine, as it turned out. In other words, it was a huge mine designed to destroy tanks. And in their little let's-blow-stuff-up minds they thought that they would be safe shooting from behind their truck. One of them eventually hit the target. As Kent described the experience, he said that the explosion and concussion were deafening. Pieces of hot metal shredded their truck, flattening their tires. All four men were struck and injured by shrapnel; one of them was lucky he did not bleed out from a shrapnel wound to his neck.

I served with other blow-'em-up-boys of the National Guard. We had come across a mortar tube and mortar rounds, all Chinese-made, during one raid, and had brought them back. The base plate didn't fit the tube but, *Hey, no worries, let's fire off some rounds anyway*! As one of the National Guardsman fired a mortar, the entire tube flew back and sent the round in an entirely different angle, over the mountain, and near a village on the other side. I could not stand the thought of it killing any of the Kouchi (gypsy) villagers living on the other side, so I hiked to the village. Fortunately, no one was hurt.

Sometimes, it is our time to go, sometimes not. Often, it is not really our time to go but we speed up the timetable. It might be a lot like when people mess up daylight savings time, and show up an hour early to church, and someone asks, "Why are you here so early?" I wonder if angels at that heavenly reception desk ponder that same question when we show up before our time. "What are you doing here?" they might ask.

There's an old saying that I saw painted on a barn along the highway in Utah: "Better late at the Golden Gate than to arrive in hell on time." Death is one time that we shouldn't worry about being late.

23: HOW TO GO

I'm not the first person to ponder death, nor the first one to contemplate when or how one dies. There is even a website, called The Darwin Awards, that is devoted to those mentally challenged folks who kill themselves in imaginative, or stupid, ways. I have almost appeared on that website, maybe a couple of times.

I was once in the Philippines on TDY (temporary duty), and I decided to go scuba diving with a group of friends. It was a last minute decision for me—I had a swimsuit, sunscreen, and towel and that's about it as far as equipment. I jumped in the van and we drove for a few hours to a beautiful area south of Manila called Batangas.

Our dive master was a young Filipino man who spoke very little English—too little to tell us that on our third dive we would need to decompress before surfacing. I was paired up with a young lady about half my size who must have used about half as much oxygen from her tanks, as it turned out. About fifteen minutes into our third dive I looked down at my gauge and noticed that I was low on air, the needle approaching the red zone—meaning I needed to be heading back to the anchor line to decompress. I looked at my partner and saw that she was still swimming around the coral. But I didn't signal for her, not wanting to bother her, and not wanting to be the first one back to the anchor line—a matter of pride.

Pride almost killed me that day, since I did not want to be the first diver to stop the dive. Unfortunately, no more than a minute later I ran completely out of air, even though my air gauge still read around

200 psi (air pressure, pounds per square inch). It was rented equipment, after all. Having no air at 75 or 80 feet down is a very depressing feeling.

My first reaction was to look at the surface of the ocean above and tell myself, *Go for it; you can make it.* Fortunately, just as I was bracing to push off the bottom, another little voice, probably from my training, convinced me otherwise. Racing for the surface, especially on the third dive of the day, can cause all kinds of funny—actually, not so funny—reactions in your body. There is the bends, which is nitrogen gas that exits into your blood stream and can cause unimaginable pain—and death. There are air embolisms that a diver may suffer if he holds his breath while ascending. The air in his lungs actually expands and wants to escape somewhere, usually through his sinuses, or eyes, chest, or other body cavities. Or you can just pass out on the way up. It's never a good thing to run out of air and try to make it to the surface.

Fortunately, I looked for my dive buddy, who was now inspecting coral a short distance away. I swam as hard as I could to reach her and made the out-of-air signal—a slash across the throat with my hand. She quickly passed an extra regulator (she had an "octopus" regulator with an extra airline) to me, and I gulped air. Oxygen never tasted so good.

The dive master eventually saw us swimming together back to the anchor line, recognized the problem, and passed me his extra airline to save the rest of my dive buddy's air. We all three hung on the anchor line for about fifteen minutes in order to decompress, which allows the nitrogen bubbles to exit your blood stream and dissipate. I had dodged Darwin. Okay, it might not have been stupid enough to qualify me for their website, but it was reckless.

But I've done stupid too. I was driving from Texas to Utah to visit my parents, especially my mother, who was suffering from cancer. During a long stretch of road through New Mexico, the children began complaining about the long drive, so I challenged them to a contest of holding our breath. We decided to see if we could hold our breath from one mile marker to another.

Unfortunately, I had been sick for a few days prior and was not feeling well. I took a few deep breaths before the marker, hyperventilating, and when we began the competition I inhaled as much as I could—I was not about to let anyone beat me, of course—and held it. I passed out, driving eighty miles per hour on cruise control.

My wife, who was also holding her breath and looking straight ahead for the next marker, eventually noticed that our vehicle was drifting to the left. *Odd,* she thought, *I wonder why he is changing lanes.* Just as we were drifting into the gravel into the median and close to crashing, she looked over at me, noticed that I was unconscious, and smacked me hard on the shoulder. Fortunately, I woke up at that point and gained control of the car.

It's never a good thing to hold your breath while ascending during a dive, nor while driving at eighty miles per hour. It is dangerous—and embarrassing.

There are embarrassing ways to die. I sometimes think about those spirits who have gone on to the next life and wonder if they ever sit around a grand campfire after they have barfed in the bucket, trading stories and discussing how they exited this one, some quite embarrassed.

"Men," starts Sgt. Rock, "I was outnumbered by a hundred enemy combatants but did not retreat. I fought to the death. It took more than one of them, and more than one bullet, to stop me."

"Way to go, GI Joe," says Genghis. "I was conquering Asia when I passed, died in a hunting accident. I admit that falling off my horse was a little embarrassing."

"We all died storming the beaches of Normandy during World Ward II, liberating France from the Nazis," others in the circle chime in.

"I climbed into a barrel and floated off Niagara Falls," says Willie—Willie Sink—from the back.

(Awkward silence.)

"Whoa," replies Genghis, "now that's embarrassing."

"We were rushing into the World Trade Towers when they were attacked, to help civilians escape," states a group of tough-looking New York police officers and firefighters.

"Hey guys, I died bungee jumping," giggles Justin—Justin Sane.

"Oh, I've heard about those bungee stick booby traps in Vietnam from some of the other veterans up here," responds Sgt. Rock angrily. There are so many Darwin Awards, and the list is growing steadily—stupid, self-inflicted, senseless deaths. Some die stupid. That said, some die worse than that: as traitors or in shame. Both are sad, but frankly, I would much rather get run over by a Boeing 747 at thirty thousand feet while flying my homemade helium balloon, fall off a zip line while traversing the Grand Canyon, or take a tumble while snowboarding down one of the pyramids. Better to die stupidly than shamefully. After a moronic death, my female family members would cry, of course, but my brothers and buddies would wipe away a tear, shake their heads, and smile. "What a character! I wonder just how fast he was going when he hit that tree?" they would question as they carried my coffin.

But I'll tell you how I really do not want to die. I do not want to dies shamefully, like one movie star did a few years back. I do not want to die of old age in prison, a traitor to my country and my family, like my colleague Aldrich Ames will. I do not want to die while betraying my wife, like another colleague. I do not want to die a traitor, criminal, or cheat. And I do not want to die hitting an Improvised Explosive donkey. My advice: if you're doing something shameful, please do not die until you stop doing it.

I'll admit, it is unrealistic to think that we can completely measure up to those that have gone before us. They were made of stout stuff. But, although we might not measure up, we can still die right. A special forces officer I worked with in Afghanistan told us before going out on an operation, "Just remember this: if shooting starts and you think you're going to die, and you feel you're going to scream like a little girl, don't . . . because you might not [die]." In other words, it's okay to die in a firefight, but do not scream like a little girl, or you will hear about it from other guys for the rest of your life.

I was thinking about Chuck Norris and how he will die, if he ever does. I will tell you how he won't die. Chuck (even his name is tough) will die while saving a group of divers from a great white shark on the Great Barrier Reef, or maybe fighting a Kodiak bear in Alaska. We might find the bear on top of Chuck, but the bear will be dead too. That's how Chuck will go out, not like a moron, or worse—a traitor.

How about this for advice—live a good life but die an even better death. If you're doing something moronic, try not to die. In Greece I rode a very powerful motorcycle that almost killed me twice. I finally decided that my wife and baby son were worth living for, and I tied a pair of his baby shoes on the handlebars to remind me not to drive like a moron.

Some of you might decide to go ahead and die a moron. If you do, at least set some kind of height or distance record while you're at it. It might not be quite as embarrassing trying to explain your early demise to the heroes sitting around that heavenly campfire.

"No, no, that's a Punji stake; I had a *bungee cord* tied to my ankles," explains Jack.

"Oh the humanity, I've never even heard of that kind of torture," moans Sgt. Rock.

"Dude, I wasn't being tortured. I actually paid other people a lot of money to tie me up by the ankles before I threw myself off a bridge."

Sgt. Rock shakes his head, slowly stands up, and leaves the campfire.

"Dang," grumbles Genghis, "and you said that you lived in America? With people like you I could have taken that continent too."

And I imagine all their wives up in that great beyond as well, sitting around their Pampered Chef party, talking about their husbands, of course. You do not want to be the subject of that unearthly conversation any more than you want to be the topic of conversations down here.

"I always warned him to stop showing off on that horse, especially when he was not out burning and plundering," complains Mrs. Khan, "but he never listened."

"Of course they don't listen," agrees Mrs. Sink. "They're all the same. Willie wasn't even wearing clean underwear, at least not when they found him at the bottom of the falls."

24: THE LAST TIME

Wouldn't it be nice to know when "the last time" really is? When will be the last time I see my wife's face? When will be the last time I ride bicycles with my sons or daughter? Or the last time I am able to speak with them? Hug them? Well, as I see it, each moment is the last, and every time is the last time.

I am not trying to be scary, but life is fragile—scary fragile. Each ride, each talk, each kiss good-bye, can be the last. Life can be over in an instant—without warning, without good-byes—*déjà through*. Your last time to see a loved one might come today—or worse, it might have been yesterday. A friend of mine, Eddie, told me that he had always intended to videotape his father and ask him to talk about his life, until his father died unexpectedly and it was too late. Immediately after Eddie left, I went to the store and bought a camcorder and videotaped my father that same day—not that long before he passed away. I filmed him just in time, before the last time.

Our son provided a lesson in how any time might be the last.

Nolan was a climber from a very early age. He could climb anything—trees, cars, furniture, fences, even appliances. Climbers climb whatever they can find, wherever they find it, whenever you are not looking. One sunny day in Greece my wife took Nolan to her friend Mary's apartment for lunch. Jacqueline and Mary enjoyed cooking and chatting while Mary's two girls and Nolan played outside on the veranda, or *retiré*, as they call it in Greece. Many penthouse apartments in Greece include a spacious terrace, which reduces the living space but affords a large area for rooftop gardens and plenty of sunshine.

Jacqueline and Mary occasionally checked on Nolan and the girls, who were not climbers, mainly to see if they needed a drink of water or a diaper change—Nolan was around eighteen months old at that time. At one point, Jacqueline walked out of the apartment and onto the terrace to see how the kids were getting along. She looked around and did not see Nolan. She felt the immediate shock that mothers experience when their child is missing—he had vanished. She searched the terrace and apartment to no avail. Nolan was gone.

The two ladies raced down the building stairwell, just in case he had been able to sneak past them and out of the apartment without their noticing—no Nolan. In a panic Jacqueline ran back out onto the rooftop terrace. Where could he be? Jacqueline's searching eyes eventually reached the other side of a fence that encircled the terrace. As her eyes followed the edge of the roof she spotted Nolan, standing on a three-foot-wide concrete ledge, with nothing between him and the road a hundred feet below—nothing but air. In fact, he was actually leaning forward, arms behind his back, casually gazing down at the cars passing below, just casually observing.

Fortunately, Jacqueline resisted the urge to scream, and she quietly called to him, trying to coax him away from the edge. The fence was actually too high for her to climb (he had done it by pushing a box next to it) and she could think of no other way to save him than to try and persuade him to come to her so she could reach over and lift him back to safety. When Nolan heard her coaxing voice he turned and started toward her but realized that she might just be trying to spoil his fun. He grinned, turned away, and ran down the ledge away from her, toward the corner of the building and the end of the ledge.

By the grace of God he did not stumble—it was probably the first time in his eighteen months that he had ever run and not fallen down. At that point Jacqueline felt desperation and helplessness to save her only child, and she screamed for Mary's husband, Steve.

Guardian angels were in there abundance that day, and one of them was Steve. Steve was a student at a Greek university and was home at that exact time, helping prepare lunch between classes. He was searching for Nolan inside the building when he heard Jacqueline scream.

Steve reacted instantly. He spotted Nolan on the ledge, raced through the apartment, and leapt over the kitchen sink and counter, straight out the window. He landed on the narrow ledge, like Spider-Man, and wrapped his arms around Nolan. I later looked at his route. I consider myself athletic but I doubt that I could have accomplished the same maneuver one out of ten times. Maybe even Steve couldn't have either—but he was able to do it that one time, when it counted.

When I got home from work hours later, Jacqueline was still crying. Her tears, however, were tears of joy and relief, thanks to Steve. We thanked him numerous times, but how can you truly thank someone for saving your son? There are no words. Years later we still have tears for Steve. Steve's family and ours left Greece about the same time—they to Chicago and we to Houston. We later heard from Steve's wife that he had passed away, much too young. Years ago, in Greece, was that last time. It was the last time that we ever saw Steve. But thanks to him, it was not our last time with Nolan. He did not die that day.

But think about it—it is not just death that snatches away our children. Our little loved ones usually do not die, but they grow up, go to school, move away from home, begin careers, join the military, get married, start their own families. And in the "twinkle of an eye" they are gone. So ask yourself, while you still have them: When is the last time that I will ever push my son on a swing? Or climb a tree together? When will be the last time I read a book with my daughter? Or tuck her in? How about hug my wife? When will be the last time I walk with her down the street, holding her hand, kissing her hair? I wish that we could all cherish each moment like it's our last—because it might be. And one day it will be.

While I was writing this very chapter my six-year-old son asked me to push him on our tree swing in our front yard. I was busy writing and almost did not go. Thank heavens that I made the right decision that time and went outside where I found him sitting on the swing, motionless, head down, looking at the grass below him, waiting—no, trusting—that I would come. As I walked up to him, he smiled and asked me philosophically, displaying a wisdom well beyond his years,

B. D. Foley

"Papa, what would I do without you? Can I push myself on this swing? Can I make my own pancakes?" *No*, I thought, *you can't, but I'll do it for you now, tomorrow, and many, many more times, I hope, until that last time.*

25: SO SMART TO BE STUPID

Zaire, or the Democratic Republic of Congo, as it is now called, will always hold a special place in my heart. It is a unique country to me because I met my wife there. I also love Zaire because the Congolese are largely a peace-loving people that want the end to their civil wars but are constantly being drawn into them. Most have little formal education but are industrious and intelligent just the same.

I often quote a major in the Congolese army, whom I met during the late 1980s. Often during breaks in training we discussed life in America, especially our justice system. After a particularly long conversation on an attempted murder of President Reagan and the case's outcome, the major had a puzzled look on his face but suddenly appeared to have found an answer to his question. He offered up a bit of philosophy, "Ah, I see; it seems to me that Americans have become so smart to be stupid."

The Congo, to me, conjures up visions of jungles, crocodiles, gorillas, and snakes. I have always loved snakes, since my early years on Snake Trail. I have loved snakes, caught snakes, and even eaten snake (python) at a restaurant in downtown Kinshasa during a first date with my wife. Even the name of the Congo's capitol, Kinshasa, sounds like a snake. It also sounds exotic: Kinshasa, Mombasa, Mufasa—remember how wonderful Mufasa sounded in that deep voice of James Earl Jones in *The Lion King*?

I once found myself on the Congo River on a powerboat. I had been invited to go waterskiing with some friends. I never dreamed that anyone would want to water-ski on the Congo. When they invited me to go with them I simply could not resist.

My other team members did resist. One of them warned me, in fact, that there were too many types of diseases and parasites one could catch in the tropical water: protozoal infections, dracunculiasis, dysentery, leptospirosis, typhoid fever, botulism, gastroenteritis, hepatitis A, cholera, river flukes, river blindness. I've read that there are even vampire fish, or candiru, in some tropical rivers that can swim up into a man's "privates" via his urine stream and implant themselves. Yes, imagine that.

I skied for a while, not even thinking about what could happen if I fell. Skiing in crocodile- and candiru-infested waters can make you an excellent skier, by the way. I did not fall once, and I managed to ski upright right up to the shore of the small island where we picnicked after I finished my run.

That would have been the end of my exposure to the water and all of the above illnesses were it not for a young skier who was having trouble getting up on his skis. Wanting to be helpful, I swam out to him and helped him position himself, pointing his skis up in the air prior to giving the "thumbs-up" for takeoff. The boat surged and the young man popped up out of the water, but he managed to make it only about twenty-five yards before he fell again. I swam out to him to help. The boat took off, and he fell again.

Eventually, he made it up out of the water and onto his skis, and the boat pulled him off into the distance, upriver. I cheered him on, but then looked around and noticed that I had floated a considerable distance downriver. The island was now much too far away to try and swim to it. And the river was about one mile across at that point. I decided to float and wait.

Waiting somewhere often gives your mind all kinds of time to think up scary thoughts. I pondered those *Tarzan* movies with crocodiles chasing Boy or Jane through the water until Tarzan dives in with a knife clenched in his teeth and kills the croc. I brought my legs in tight against my chest, in an "anti-crocodile" position, kind of like the "anti-eel" position, which I already knew, trying to not offer any bite-sized appendages. I then thought about the river flukes that my colleague had warned against, and kept my head up in the air to avoid the brown water from splashing into my mouth.

Then the thought of candiru fish entered my mind. For some reason, candiru fish scare me much more than a crocodile. I think that many men would agree. A baseball to the crotch might be funny, but not a vampire fish. I adopted an even tighter, curled-up-in-a-ball anti-vampire-fish position and fiercely resisted the urge to pee, which is not easy, because we all know that men pee when we swim. But not in the bathtub.

I probably didn't float for as long as it seemed, which was like an eternity. People on shore eventually remembered that I had disappeared downriver and sent the boat to pick me up and return me to shore. I was cured of any more desire to ski the Congo and did not get back into the water. I learned later that there are no candiru fish in Africa—it is native to the Amazon. I also learned that it is illegal to import them into the United States. That would be so stupid to be stupid.

26: CREATURES OF HABIT

Habits are a double-edged sword. Good habits can turn into motor-memory skills that might save your life, like during a combat situation. Just the habit of "tap-rack-bang" (when the firearm misfires or jams, tap the magazine to seat it, rack another round in the chamber, and fire) can be lifesaving. Habits of not pointing a firearm at anyone you do not wish to kill, or keeping your finger off the trigger until you are ready to fire, can also mean the difference between life and death. I used to touch my hip every time I left the house, without even thinking, to make sure my sidearm was strapped on. Those are all good habits.

Bad habits, however, can be just as influential in a bad way to a young man.

It's hard not to pick up bad habits as we age. We might start biting our fingernails (yep, did that), picking our nose (try not to), speeding on the freeway (not anymore), riding a bike without a helmet (stopped that), yelling at our kids (working on that), playing video games (stopped that), eating Cheetos (stopped that), and any of a million other habits.

Charles Duhigg wrote about habits in his book *The Power of Habit*. He includes a story of a soldier he met while serving as a newspaper reporter in Baghdad, Iraq, who figured out how to stop riots in a town called Kufa, near his base. The major analyzed videotapes of riots and identified a pattern: "Violence was usually preceded by a crowd of Iraqis gathering in a plaza or open space. . . . Food vendors would show up, as well as spectators." The major met with the mayor of Kufa and asked that they keep food vendors out of the plazas. The food vendors stopped attending, the crowds grew restless and hungry, and when they couldn't find food they went home. Habit broken.

"Understanding habits is the most important thing I've learned in the army," remarked the major. "It's changed everything about how I see the world. You want to fall asleep fast and wake up feeling good? Pay attention to your nighttime patterns and what you automatically do when you get up. You want to make running easy? Create triggers to make it a routine. I drill my kids on this stuff. My wife and I write out habit plans for our marriage. This is all we talk about in command meetings. Not one person in Kufa would have told me that we could influence crowds by taking away the kebab stands, but once you see everything as a bunch of habits, it's like someone gave you a flashlight and a crowbar and you can get to work."

Duhigg argues that habits are first created from cravings. He writes, "One researcher at Cornell, for instance, found how powerfully food and scent cravings can affect behavior when he noticed how Cinnabon stores were positioned inside shopping malls." (Remember those doughnut stores I wrote about earlier?) "Most food sellers locate their kiosks in food courts, but Cinnabon tries to locate their stores away from the food stalls. Why? Because Cinnabon executives want the smell of cinnamon rolls to waft down hallways and around corners uninterrupted, so that shoppers will start sub-consciously craving a roll. By the time a consumer turns a corner and sees the Cinnabon store, that craving is a roaring monster inside his head and he'll reach, unthinkingly, for his wallet. The habit loop is spinning because a sense of craving has emerged."

Cravings, and habits, can cause a man to reach for his wallet, or a bag of Cheetos, or a video game remote, often subconsciously. Smells trigger our arm to reach for a wallet, almost without thinking. Chimes for an email cause us to forget about our studies—or writing a book—and move our mouse to our email account.

But there is hope. We can replace these bad habits with good ones. We can replace overeating with exercise. Replace porn with sports. Duhigg provides hope and a solution. "Anyone can use this basic formula to create habits of her or his own. Want to exercise more?

Choose a cue, such as going to the gym as soon as you wake up, and a reward, such as a smoothie after each workout. Then think about that smoothie, or about the endorphin rush you'll feel. Allow yourself to anticipate the reward. Eventually, that craving will make it easier to push through the gym doors every day."

Cue, reward, routine. Cue, reward, routine. That's how it's done. That's how alcoholics stop drinking and how those addicted to pornography stop looking at vulgar images: by identifying cues and rewards "that encourage their alcoholic habits" and creating new routines and new habit loops.

I had habits in the CIA. I might have had habits that saved my life and I didn't even know it. I routinely watched vehicles behind me, identifying those that took the same turns as me and counting those turns. I noticed other subway passengers who entered and exited at the same stops. I changed my route to and from work, going at different times, returning home earlier or later. These small actions all became habits, small subconscious decisions that might have saved my life, without my even knowing it.

Habits can save a young man's life literally, or more than likely, figuratively. A habit of getting out of bed in the morning at the same time, making his bed, reading the news instead of playing a video game, eating a handful of healthy nuts instead of a box full of doughnuts, filling out an online application instead of watching online smut, can make all the difference for him and might save his life.

I will end with one last suggestion from Duhigg. Belief makes a difference. Belief is an ingredient in changing and reworking our habit loops. A belief in God, humanity, yourself, or the idea that something good is out there is crucial. "Belief seems critical," he adds. "You don't have to believe in God, but you do need the capacity to believe that things will get better."

Life—with its challenges and pitfalls and disappointments—happens. You will flunk a test and then find yourself walking through a mall, smell cinnamon rolls, and then reach for your wallet. You might be going through a divorce, be missing your young son or daughter or wife, and fall back into a bad habit. You might find yourself in Afghanistan, sick for days with a terrible illness, puking and suffering from dysentery, and fall back into a bad habit. Just believe that things will get better. Believe that you are a child of God. If you do not believe in God, then just hope that there is someone somewhere who loves you or will love you.

Just believe. Believe that the sun will come up tomorrow. Believe that you can overcome your bad habits and create good ones. And that will make all the difference.

27: GET A JOB

Remember back in Chapter 13, when I told you that CIA operatives will search out targets who have vulnerabilities and then manipulate them based upon that vulnerability? Well, that was a lie.

What, did you seriously think that you could believe everything you read? In a book? On the Internet? Bwaahhhhh!

Okay, it was not really a lie but a half-truth. I'll now tell you the whole truth: CIA operations officers target sources based upon vulnerabilities, yes, but *recruit them based upon motivation*. That is how espionage works. An operations officer finds a target with a vulnerability. He then turns that vulnerability into motivation, recruits the target, and gathers intelligence.

I always wanted to chuckle when I heard expressions such as "gathering intelligence," or "intelligence gatherers," almost like we were out gathering flowers in a field! To be clear, I did not "gather" intelligence. I stole it. It is "intelligence stealing," and I was an "intelligence thief."

Now that we have cleared that up.

How can an operations officer turn someone's vulnerability into a motivation? Simple: by flipping his perspective. By having him look for a solution rather than focusing on the vulnerability or problem. That might sound a bit simplistic, but it is true. And you can do it for yourself, too. You can take whatever vulnerability you have and turn it into a positive, motivational drive. You can follow the words of Bing Crosby in his famous song, "You got to accentuate the positive, eliminate the negative . . ."

And you can do it when it comes to improving grades at school, gaining more playing time on a sports team, or finding a job.

To succeed, you first need to recruit yourself. You must take those vulnerabilities—which we all have—and turn them into motivations. You must do it as sure as we recruit sources in the CIA, by convincing yourself that you can go after a goal and that you can attain it.

For instance:

—You don't have money? That is a vulnerability, to feel poor. It can be depressing and discouraging, and it can even make you want to do stupid stuff. But you can turn that depressing vulnerability into a motivation: Let's go get some money so I can enjoy the activities/travel/car/my own place (insert your goal) that I want and deserve.

—You feel like you are wasting your life and have no direction? Let's find a career/passion/destination for life, something to help you feel motivated to get up in the morning, make your bed, and eat pancakes!

—You feel lonely? Let's find a friend/girlfriend/wife, someone with whom you can find friendship, companionship, and fulfillment.

So first of all, identify your vulnerability and then change it into a motivation. Manipulate yourself, master yourself, recruit yourself.

Next, after you have found your motivations, or goals, make them specific and realistic.

Specific: In the CIA we either targeted based upon our own needs and observations or had officers at our headquarters who were specifically trained and assigned to targeting. They would usually research where our government had intelligence gaps and then find ways to fill those gaps. Most often, operations officers played a big part in assessing sources and matching up what they could provide with what we needed. This targeting drilled down to specifically what intelligence a source could provide. We then made goals: long-term and short-term goals, even goals for each meeting. We never met with a source without a list of requirements or specific intelligence dealing with the who, what, when, why, and where.

Realistic: We would not ask a source who worked in a hotel to provide intel on what a president's views were on a United Nations resolution. Neither should you ask yourself to become a brain surgeon, at least not over the coming year. Your goals must be attainable, if for no other reason than that you do not want to set yourself up for failure. Unrealistic demands of a source, or asset, can lead to him being arrested as he struggles to fulfill them. Unrealistic demands on yourself are just as damaging. Do not set the bar so high that you cannot realistically jump over it.

Prioritized: My list of requirements for sources was usually on a list of urgency. Prioritize your goals in the same way. Do you really need that new hoverboard or latest cell phone, or can you get by without until you have a car and your own apartment? Should you pay your heating bill first, before you fly to Aruba? These are called "opportunity costs": when you spend money on one item, you lose the "opportunity" to pay for another. If you spend your check on a new gaming system, you will not have the opportunity to pay for your training, for your next job, or for your apartment.

Next, assess yourself. Back to the "bread and butter" of CIA work: assessing and examining what someone knows, what their strengths and weaknesses are, what makes them tick, what they fear, what they love. Assessment is a skill, but self-assessment is probably more an art, and it is not easy. It is difficult to admit our mistakes, our inadequacies, and our fears, but it is the path to enlightenment, as Chinese philosopher Lao-Tzu noted.

How to assess yourself? You might start by asking your mother—who is probably the person who knows you best—or father, relative, teacher, or good friend. Ask them to tell you what you enjoy doing or what you are good at doing and what skills you possess. Take notes and ponder what they say. Ask them about your abilities (natural talents), skills (something you have learned), and interests (something you enjoy, like fishing, sports, and so on). Then add the qualities you know about yourself, and make a list.

Next, match your qualities (abilities, skills, interests) with a career field. Begin looking for job opportunities, starting from the broad (for example agriculture, manufacturing, restaurant industries) and then narrowing it down to a specific position you might be interested in (livestock, flower nursery, welder, cook). If you need training for a particular position, go after it; get it.

Then it is time to get the job.

—First, find a job opening. Look for "Now Hiring" signs, search the Internet, visit a job services office or a trade schools, go to the library, and ask friends, family, and neighbors, especially those who work in your desired field. There are jobs out there.

—Fill out an application. Be tidy. Be honest. If you've been fired, tell them the truth, but explain why you are different now, what you have learned, how you have changed. Tell them that it would never happen again, because it won't, because you won't let it happen again. Fill out the application with a pen. If the employer will let you take an application home, take two: fill out the first one as scratch, or work copy, and the second one perfectly to present to them. A crucial part of the job hunt is the interview, or the ops meeting, as we call it in the CIA. This where the rubber hits the road, make or break, as they say. This is when we recruit that employer.

When you arrive (early!), dressed nicely (better to overdress than underdress), remember three things: 1) greeting ("Good morning"), 2) introduce yourself ("My name is . . ."), 3) state the purpose of your visit ("I'm here to see Mrs. . . ."), then wait for a response. 1-2-3, then wait.

Look around while you wait. See what she has on the wall or on her desk. When I decided to transfer from the DI (Directorate of Intelligence) to the DO (Directorate of Operations), I interviewed with the branch chief, a large man named Bill, who would decide whether they needed me or not. As I sat in his office waiting for his arrival, I noticed a painting on his wall of rugby players in a scrum. At the time, I was playing with a local rugby club. When Bill entered the room we exchanged greetings and, when I found an opening, I asked him about the painting. He immediately became more animated and asked if I played the game, to which I responded that I was on the Washington Rugby Club. He sat back and exclaimed, "That's my old club!" As you might guess, most of the rest of the interview was spent discussing positions, win-loss records, injuries, and such. I got the job, maybe based upon my qualifications, but also because I noticed a painting on the wall.

Build rapport. More espionage. Rapport building includes identifying commonalities—such as common interests or backgrounds—and making connections. It is necessary in finding a girlfriend, a spouse, and even a job, like I was able to do with Bill. When the interviewer asks you where you are from, tell her and then ask her the same question. Use elicitation ploys (chapter 11).

Listen. Actively listen, which means to concentrate, provide feedback, engage, nod your head, and maybe say, "Yes, um-hmm," from time to time, to show that you are listening. Interact with the interviewer.

Do not overshare. In the CIA it was dangerous to overshare, especially with sharks swimming around that can smell blood in the water—weaknesses. It is not a good idea to tell a Russian SVR officer (used to be called KGB) that you are mad at being passed over for promotion or that your car has broken down and you don't have enough money for repairs, nor is it a good idea to volunteer to an employer that you did not get very good grades in school or to talk about your religion, your political affiliation, your living situation, what you did over the weekend, or that you enjoy blowing up neighbors' mailboxes. Tell the employer what she needs to know and no more. Oh, and stop blowing up mailboxes.

Take a notebook with a list of points you want to bring up, such as your experience and skills. You might also include questions you have for them regarding the company to show that you have been doing some homework, such as "How long have you been in business? What is your business outlook is for the coming year? Are there opportunities for advancement? What training will I receive?" Do not ask about salary or vacation time, especially not early on in an interview.

Be prepared. Practice potential questions with a family member, such as "Why do you want to work here" (No, the answer is not "so I can pay my rent!"), "Why do you have a gap in your employment," "What are your strengths and weaknesses," or "What did you do on your last job?" Rehearse the answers, even practice by yourself in front of the mirror, and then try it with family or friends.

Ask for help. Men often won't ask for directions at a gas station. They won't ask for advice, for encouragement, or for help in a difficult situation if they are being bullied, trying to overcome a bad habit, or feeling depressed. Do not be embarrassed to ask for help. We are all in this "boat" together. Get advice from someone who has done that job before, interviewed before, or worked in that exact factory where you want to work. No need to go it alone.

At the end of the interview, ask when they will be making their decision. This little question can save you days or weeks of worry.

Stay hopeful. My biggest, best recruitment of my career in the CIA took two years, from genesis to conclusion. Two years. That is a long time. It might take you some time to get the job you want. Be patient, but most importantly maintain hope. Never lose hope.

If you are not hired (and none of us are hired to every job), ask if you may apply again in the future, then ask if they know of another business in the area that is hiring. This will accomplish two things: they might know of another firm that is hiring, but they will also note the determination that you have, and they might keep your application on file. You will make a great last impression.

If you get the job, congratulations! You have successfully recruited the boss. Now, once you have it, keep it by working as hard as you can, showing initiative in terms of doing what is asked of you and more. Be responsible. Be early to work. Don't be the first one out the door at the end of the day. Be a team player. Don't criticize the boss in front of others. Be loyal to the company.

My dad, a retired air force pilot, warned me when I began my career at the CIA to not be tempted by that feeling of "entitlement." He was right. It can be particularly tempting to think that way in the CIA with all the "toys"—night-vision equipment, firearms, body armor, sunglasses—floating around. A feeling of entitlement can also be the fastest avenue to getting fired. One officer in the CIA thought he was not being promoted fast enough or earning enough money. He grew a sense of entitlement, so he decided to create bogus sources, write bogus intelligence that he gleaned from the newspaper, and then pocket the imaginary sources' salary payments. It eventually caught up with him, and he lost his dream job. Do not feel entitled.

Then buy what you worked so hard to earn—your car, a down payment on a home—and save the rest. Save for your future travel, your future spouse, your future children. Maybe give some to charity. But put some aside for a rainy day. Because it will rain.

Think about what you want in life, and then decide what it is. Then manipulate, motivate, and recruit yourself based upon that desire. You are your own best operations officer.

28: MARIA

I lied when I said that I cannot give you secret X-ray glasses. There is such a thing, in a way.

In *The Bourne Identity*, Jason Bourne does not remember who he is but gradually discovers that he has incredible observation skills. While sitting in a rest stop cafe during one scene, he tells Marie, the young woman played by Franka Potente, who has been embroiled in his escape and is trying to help him, "I can tell you the license plate numbers of all six cars outside. I can tell you that our waitress is left-handed, and that the guy sitting up at the counter weighs 215 pounds and knows how to handle himself. I know the best place to look for a gun is the cab of the gray truck outside. And at this altitude, I can run flat out for a half-mile before my hands start shaking. Now, why would I know that?"

Okay, it's a movie. I could never run flat out for a half-mile. And the CIA never inserted electronic tracking transmitters in my body—not any that I know of, anyway. But, the point is, observation skills play a huge part in being a secret agent man. And, guess what! Observation skills play a huge part in being a gentleman as well.

Now, you might be expecting some cool spy story to show how observation skills saved my life. The truth is, most of us sit in a cafe and don't observe anything more than whether our bacon is too crispy or whether the waitress is attractive.

I will tell you a story, however. I will tell you about a little girl named Maria.

149

Like I said, I often visited Athens, Greece. The city can be congested, oppressive, and smoggy, and that is sometimes difficult to tolerate, especially when you are trying to navigate through massive traffic jams. When our visits extended over a weekend my family, along with most of the Athenians, searched for activities in the countryside outside of Athens, whether along the coast of the Mediterranean Sea or up in the mountains.

On weekends when we could not escape the city, my wife, my son, and I often visited an orphanage for disabled children on the northern edge of Athens. The facility, called PikPah (which is an acronym for the Greek name), housed many children who had been partially or totally abandoned by their parents. They had all manner of disabilities, both mental and physical challenges. They were the most disadvantaged of their society, yet, paradoxically, they were some of the happiest, most loving children you could ever meet.

Life at the orphanage would have been unimaginable to an American child accustomed to all of the luxuries of life in America, such as having his own room, iPad, iPhone, Xbox, and sometimes even his own sports car to drive to high school. The PikPah children's possessions were limited to a bed and a few personal items they could fit into a small nightstand. Some thirty children were crammed into one barracks-style building.

Their physical needs were taken care of, but not much else. Some of the nurses were obviously loving and caring, but others were not as compassionate. During Christmas season one year, missionaries provided new sweat suits for each child. A week later, most of the clothes had gone "missing." When we asked about their new clothes, the children reported, in hushed voices, that the staff had taken them from all but the larger children who were able to defend themselves. It was very sad.

Over time, we developed close relationships with several of the children. Vangellis was around twelve years of age and weighed maybe fifty pounds, with terribly skinny arms that hung lifelessly from his shoulders, a tiny body with a giant spirit. Nikos, confined to a wheelchair, had nothing in terms of earthly possessions, yet he would rarely ask for anything from us. Stavros never left the ward, never left his bed in fact, yet we never saw him depressed or without a smile on his face. And then there was Maria. I will tell you about Maria.

During most visits we would simply chat with the children, play with them, or hug, feed, and love them. Regularly we would ask if we could bring them anything from the *periptero*, a small kiosk store located at the bottom of the hill below the facility. One of the children, usually Maria, would make the rounds, asking each child in her soft voice if they would like something: chewing gum (especially the packages with soccer player cards), a soda, or maybe a magazine. This was often a highlight for the children.

And always, before departing, we would be asked the same question: "When will you come back again?" This was a torturous question for me, as I hesitated to promise when I would, or could, return. They unfailingly remembered when we had promised to come, and would mildly scold me if we missed a day. They always remembered.

On one occasion, I had driven to the orphanage by myself on my motorcycle. They loved it when I brought my motorcycle because I would sometimes sit them on the seat in front of me and give them rides around the parking circle. After greetings and some conversation with the children I asked Maria what she would like me to purchase from the kiosk. She soon returned with the list and softly told me that she had asked everyone and had made a list. Much like Nikos, she had omitted anything for herself, but I eventually elicited her order. When I saw the rather lengthy list I jokingly, and carelessly, as it turned out, remarked that I would be broke from purchasing so many items. I then took the list from her, hopped on my motorcycle, made the short trip to the kiosk, and then returned to the ward.

I walked past the nurses' station and into the children's room and began passing out the candy, small toys, and magazines to the children. As I was doing this, Maria, with a rather concerned expression on her face, approached me, asked me to open my hand, and then placed a pile of Greek coins—drachmas—on my palm. I was understandably surprised and asked her why she was giving me money. She responded that she was worried about me not having any money after buying them treats and gifts. When she had learned that I was "broke," she had immediately gone around the room again, only this time to tell the other children that I was in trouble and needed money.

What else could I do but put my arm around her shoulder and try to hold back tears? I was overcome by so much love from a little girl. I managed to choke out that I could not take the money and that I was not broke but had spoken in jest.

Now why would I tell you about Maria when discussing observation skills? Because she was as good as or better than Jason Bourne. She listened attentively and snatched that one little word that flew out of my mouth. Then, after observing and listening, she acted upon it immediately.

How many of us are that observant? Most of us go through life in a daze or haze of distractions, thinking of ourselves, our discomforts, or our selfish desires. How many of us men hear someone else complain about their life, that their parents are getting divorced, that they have no money to go to the prom, or that they no longer want to live, while we sit and daydream of the gym, homework that we need to do, or the newest Warcraft video game?

Do we even look at the person? Do we really listen to what she is saying? More importantly, do we think about what she is implying? What is she hinting?

Men do not understand that women do not just talk; they communicate. Their feelings, wishes, desires, dreams, are often hidden in the words where we need to find them. Women are actually testing us, or vetting us, wanting to know if we will make the effort to concentrate and decipher their words.

"Do I look fat in this dress?" is not a question about the dress. She wants to know if you find her attractive, if you love her.

"Do you think that woman across the restaurant is attractive?" is not a question about that other woman. Your girlfriend, or wife, wants to know if you love her, and only her, and will not cheat on her with some other woman.

It is up to us to listen to her words, yes, but also to look into her eyes, see what she is feeling, feel what she is feeling, and communicate. And then we need to act, like Maria did.

If a small girl of ten or eleven and all those other orphan children who gave her money for me, with all their challenges, having abandoned by their families, with nothing in terms of material possessions, can be so observant and unselfish, then so can we. Sure, try to memorize the license plate numbers of several vehicles in a parking lot or see if the waitress is left-handed. Use your secret X-ray glasses—or observation skills. But more importantly notice if your girlfriend, your spouse, your friend, or a stranger, is feeling sad, lonely, or even suicidal. Notice if someone needs help or protection or is short on money or short of friends.

Observe like Jason Bourne, but act like Maria.

29 : MIKE

A t one time I worked with five "Mikes," all in the same office. Most of them were solid guys. I imagine that Mikes are like anyone else: Franks, Joes, Herbs. What's in a name? But these Mikes were interesting—interesting that they could share the same name, profession, and office—but not much else. Let me tell you about them.

One was Maniacal Mike. He was a bit crazy. We were both slated to go to Europe and were enrolled in language classes. Before long, Mike started missing classes. He informed the instructors that he was being called away on a "mission" for HQ. We all wondered how he was going to learn a very difficult language, being gone so much. I was also wondering how I was going to survive a tour with him and his craziness. Fortunately, I needn't have worried.

After a few weeks of skipped classes, the dean of the school called up headquarters to complain. They informed her that they had not pulled him away and that he should be attending classes. When the Dean informed them that Maniacal Mike had disappeared, they began an investigation. The security officer who was assigned to the case, Ed, was a friend of mine. He told me that he went to Maniacal Mike's house to speak with the wife, asking her where he was. She told Ed, in an insulting tone, that it was unbelievable that Ed—and the entire agency—was not aware that her husband had gone "overseas on a secret mission." Ed just smiled, nodded, and walked away.

Ed then began interviewing folks at the language school. *Have you seen Mike?* After some prodding, a couple of the students learning

Arabic informed Ed that Maniacal Mike and the wife of an outgoing COS (Chief of Station) had been cozying up in the cafeteria. Ed decided to go visit the wife at her hotel to ask her about the missing employee.

"Do you know where we might find Mike?" he asked.

"How would I know where he is?" she replied angrily.

"Just a hunch. Is he here?" he insisted.

"How dare you insinuate that! He is not here," she shot back.

Ed couldn't take it anymore, so he called toward the back room, "Mike, you better come to the office tomorrow and we'll talk." He only had to wait for a moment before a faint voice answered from the back room, "Okay." Maniacal Mike showed up the next day and was forced to resign. Last I heard, he had left the CIA and was working as a mercenary somewhere in the Middle East, training some group that was trying to overthrow a government. And they had hired Maniacal Mike—former military special forces, SWAT, paratrooper, underwater demolition, DEA, PTA . . . and CIA.

Another Mike—we'll call him Married Mike—was as devoted as Maniacal Mike was disloyal. One trip, Mike and I roomed together to save money. I found out that he would travel with an eight-by-ten-inch picture of his baby boy, Michael Jr., and keep it on his hotel room nightstand. I seem to recall a photo of his wife on the nightstand, but not nearly as large. Married Mike used to look at that picture every night before he slept. He loved Jr. and he loved to talk about Jr., so I knew everything about Jr.—how much he weighed, growth charts, ear infections, what kind of diapers and formulas were best, and his first words.

And he had the annoying habit of cooing at every little baby—especially baby boys—in restaurants, hotels, sidewalks, and in the airport, patting them on the head, asking the parents the age of the child, bringing up Michael Jr., of course. Married Mike missed that little boy and his wife so much during our travels. I used to think that he talked about his family too much until I got married, had a baby boy, and started telling everyone that would listen about my sons diapers diapers, his ear infections, and when he first said "Papa."

Married Mike also had the annoying habit of bragging about the Jersey Shore, even while we were lying on the beach in Mombasa, Kenya. "Oh, this is nothing like the Jersey Shore," he would boast. "The Jersey Shore has much nicer sand; it's tons better." The Jersey Shore has a boardwalk. The Jersey Shore has this and that. I thought Married Mike was up in the night, as my dad used to say, until I visited the Jersey Shore and found out he was right. It beats Mombasa.

Married Mike had another weakness. He was not the best driver, and he was as terrible at directions as he was devoted as a husband and father. He could hardly drive in a straight line, let alone handle the many roundabouts around Nairobi. I'll give it to him that round-abouts are difficult enough to navigate in Australia, let alone the chaos of Nairobi. But Married Mike just couldn't wrap his head around the concept of remaining in your lane as you go around the circle. He would either cut straight across the circle, changing lanes as he went, or drift to the outside. And he did it all while screaming at other drivers, "Hey, hey, hey, get out of the way—whoa, whoa, what in the world are you doing?!"

It was nerve-racking to let him drive, but my other colleagues and I could not offend him by not giving him a turn to drive. So we would toss him the keys—and our lives. And it finally happened. He was driving around the circle and yelling at the other drivers, "Hey, hey, hey, where are you going?" us with our eyes closed, when he sideswiped a car. He got out, angry at the other driver, who checked his vehicle and tried to identify which of the many scratches down the side of his junk was the most recent and caused by us. We eventually all got back into our vehicles and continued on our way.

I got even with Married Mike. We visited another safari park located just on the outskirts of Nairobi. We drove around until we spotted a large lion, sitting and sunning on the grass. Married Mike was driving well that day and did not run over the lion—he parked about fifteen yards away. We watched for a little while—until I decided to terrify him as much as he had terrified me in traffic. I opened the door and began to get out. Married Mike looked at me and began the "Hey, hey, hey, what are you doing?" comments, in his New York accent. I exited the vehicle and began to walk slowly around the door, toward the front of the vehicle, and closer to the lion. Married Mike began moaning and groaning while he watched me, and he pled for me to get back into our land rover. I replied that I was fine—not to worry, the lion even appeared sleepy. I continued to walk until suddenly the lion's head snapped around and I saw his large golden eyes staring at me. I was back in the car in a flash. That was enough teasing for one day.

Another was called Miserly Mike. He was our logistics (logs) officer—and a good one. But he no longer wanted to be our logs officer—he wanted to be a training officer like the rest of us. He watched us come and go, visiting far-off lands, returning with tans in the winter and armed with all kinds of gifts, daggers, swords, stories, and books of American Express traveler's checks—leftover per diem money. You see, Uncle Sam gave us per diem money—funds for room and board during the trip—and we were allowed to stay where we wanted and keep what was left over.

I was famous in the office for finding the cheapest, scariest, most disgusting hotels imaginable. I once stayed in a hotel in Cairo, Egypt, that scared even me when I first saw it. It had an eerie resemblance to the toymaker's building in the *Blade Runner* movie. You know the building: big, old, exposed elevator shaft running down the center, rain dripping down through the roof. Except it wasn't raining. It cost me eight dollars a night, which included two meals. I actually splurged a little, upgrading to a room with its own bathroom—twelve dollars a night.

The day finally came for Miserly Mike's promotion to training officer, which meant that he could now travel to exotic places and return with a tan, stories, and buckets of per diem money. The only thing—the CIA, in its infinite wisdom, changed the system soon after Miserly Mike was promoted to one that rendered all per diem money accountable. That meant that he would not be able to stay in a disgusting old hotel and pocket the difference. He could either stay in the nice hotel and spend it all, or stay in the dump and give back the rest.

Miserly Mike was incensed but determined to make money anyhow—somehow. He first reckoned that he could save some money on the meals portion of the per diem. He began skipping meals, trying to get by on one meal a day. He still returned from his trips tanned, but twenty or so pounds lighter. Then he figured that he could make up more of the difference by collecting shampoo packets, soaps, toilet paper, and probably towels from the hotels. He got the reputation for taking about anything that wasn't nailed down. One evening he was sitting on a beautiful couch in a hotel lobby and began admiring the plush cushions. "No, Mike, don't even think about it," our colleagues pleaded. The cushions were missing the next morning.

This was before the days of eBay, so we do not know what Miserly Mike did with all of his hotel plunder. But I always imagined him sitting at some flea market selling his shampoo packets, soaps, and cushions, kind of a miniature Bed Bath & Beyond. Sadly, he was eventually transferred to another office—a few months before the government returned to the old, non-accountable per diem system.

We also worked with a guy I will call Misinformed Mike. This Mike traveled with my wife and I and another colleague to Haiti. As I mentioned, it was not a safe area, so we decided to "procure" some firearms. Tom, another member of the team, and I were issued side-arms. Oddly, Misinformed Mike declined, stating, "I do not want a gun." Tom and I looked at each other and agreed, "Fine, while they are chopping you up that will give us time to escape." Misinformed Mike did not much like that idea, but commented, "No, I will just talk my way out of any conflict." Only problem—Misinformed Mike did not speak a word of French, let alone Haitian French (pidgin). In fact, his Spanish language was so bad that he was often assigned an interpreter in Latin America to translate his version of Spanish into understandable Spanish.

Last and not least, we worked with a Mixed Martial Arts (MMA) Mike. I could tell you more about MMA Mike, but that wouldn't be real smart, would it?

30: ROCKS TO RIFLES

Boys have loved weapons since the beginning of time—in every culture, and in every country of the world. It begins at an early age. Boys look on the ground, see a rock, and immediately look for something or someone at which to throw it. We know that boys have extra genes and the Y chromosome. It would only make sense that we have an as yet undetected "R chromosome," for rocks and rifles.

My sons Nolan and Brandon were both born loving rocks. Neither can walk down a trail without picking up rocks, throwing rocks, or putting the shiny ones in their pockets. They especially love to throw rocks in the water and skip rocks. When Nolan was younger, he would throw them every chance he could. He nailed his first victim—a middle-aged friend of the family—in the head with a fist-sized rock when he was around three years old. It was a pretty impressive throw. It would have been better if he had hit her husband in the crotch. Now that would have been hilarious.

I enjoyed rocks as a kid. I was even a "rock hound" and loved to search for fossils, gypsum, petrified rock, and arrowheads in the mountains around southern Utah. I would pride myself in being able to throw the farthest and most accurately of all the boys in the neighborhood. Forty-something years later I had a rock-throwing contest with a contingent of Afghan soldiers and beat all but one of them. He could really throw.

Rock throwing eventually morphs into other forms of weaponry. My brothers and I shifted to rubber band guns at around the age of six. We shot cardboard for maybe five minutes until we realized that we should be shooting moving targets. Grasshoppers were plentiful in the garden and in an empty lot next to our house, and we honed our skills on them. I soon was able to shoot them out of the air, although my brothers dispute that.

Next came BB guns. My father gave me my first BB gun, a Daisy, when I was about eight or nine. I shot everything I could find with that gun: cans, bottles, fence posts, and lizards. My brothers and I—armed with our BB guns—even killed a rattlesnake. We were proud of ourselves for getting him before he got us.

I remember taking hunter safety, but I don't know if any of it actually sunk in. My brothers, friends, and I wore shop goggles and had BB gun wars in Ramón's sugar beet field until he kicked David in the butt. We would low-crawl through the rows and shoot each other until we couldn't take the pain anymore. There's something fascinating, and very funny, for a boy to be able to launch a projectile at a target, watch that target hop up and down, and listen to him howl, especially if you shoot him in the crotch. It's science, or physics. "To every action there is an equal and opposite reaction." And it's that R chromosome and the extra M chromosome that many boys also have—M for mean.

At around twelve we moved on to .22 caliber rifles and hunting jackrabbits in "the valley" sagebrush. Pump .22s can spit out a lot of bullets—some people call it "pray and spray." I don't remember hitting many rabbits with my rifle. Sometimes I got lucky, and other times I was not so lucky. One day I chased a rabbit around in a circle, spraying rounds after him. When we returned home my dad called me outside. He was standing at the rear of his old Suburban panel truck.

"Come here," Dad called, "I'd like to show you something."

"What?" I asked.

"Do you see anything different about the back of my truck?" he questioned.

"Nope."

"What about that hole in the tailgate? Doesn't it look a lot like a bullet hole to you?"

"Oh. Maybe."

"Be a little more careful about where you are shooting," he cautioned.

I think that he went easy on me because of his experience with guns. He told us that he and his brothers did some target practice with their .22 calibers in a back alley behind their house in Moberly, Missouri. They didn't realize that their rounds were going past the cans, through a garage door, and into the back end of a neighbor's vehicle—turning the rear end into Swiss cheese. And then there were all those Japanese military transport vehicles that he had shot up from his B-25 bomber during World War II. He had no choice but to show some understanding for one little bullet hole.

I graduated to 12-gauge shotguns when I was in junior high. I shot so many shells that my shoulder would hurt for a couple of days. Eventually that got kind of boring, hunting rabbits that couldn't shoot back. My brothers, friends, and I were usually spread out in a long line, probably 75 yards apart. I'm not sure who was the first one to do it, but the next thing we knew, we were shooting at each other—à la Dick Cheney. We found that we could yell "incoming" as a warning, and lob "shot" at each other from a distance, as long as the "target" remembered to turn the other way, bend over, and cover his ears.

Jackrabbits are in abundance in southern Utah. We mainly shot rabbits because they were a moving target and because they were a nuisance to the farmers. I eventually grew tired of it—and even a little disgusted. One day after school, I went out hunting by myself. I had shot nine rabbits in no time and figured that I'd reach ten and stop. Unfortunately, when I shot my tenth rabbit, I realized that I was out of shells. And when I walked up to the rabbit, I saw that it was only injured, flopping around. My only option was to stomp it to death. I've never enjoyed rabbit hunting since then.

Some men learn to suppress the R chromosome. Not my brother Craig. He loves guns, holsters, ammunition, and all the accouterments. His nieces and nephews call me "Uncle Fun," and they call him "Uncle Gun." Everyone knows some man who has a runaway R chromosome. They even have their own language. Craig speaks "gun" fluently. He was talking to me the other day about going to Cabela's and getting some ".556s." I figured he was talking about Levi jeans and told him that he had enough pairs to last a lifetime. He sounded a little disgusted as he informed me that he was talking about ammunition, not jeans.

Craig has a hard time accepting the fact that his brother is not more enthusiastic about guns. I think that he figured that I'd be cured of my "recessive R gene" when I traveled to the war zones. After every trip, he would quiz me relentlessly on all the guns I came across. "What kinds of guns did you shoot? What did you carry daily? The NATO round? How many rounds in a magazine? The one with the collapsible stock?" I'd usually answer something like, "I don't know, it was black and kind of long." It drove him crazy.

I guess I look at guns more like a tool than my dependent—as some guys do. I like shovels, rakes, saws, and drills. And I don't expect Craig to worship them the way I do. I do not force my beliefs on him. I don't ask Craig every time he visits a farm, "What type of shovels did you see? Any hammers? What do you carry? Man, I wish that I had that new Fat Max Extreme 28-ounce hammer with shock dampening core, torque-stabilizing bars, and magnetic nail starter!"

I'm surprisingly ambivalent about guns for a former firearms instructor. I'm a decent shot with pistols or rifles, but I just don't enjoy firing them. A friend once tried to talk me into spending Saturdays with him at shooting competitions. I went once and tried to enjoy it but couldn't, probably also because I wasn't that good at it. I figured that it was not worth either all that time away from home or the money. And I especially don't like cleaning guns after shooting.

Training marksmanship overseas was an experience. A big part of my four years spent as a trainer was teaching military and police how to shoot. I went to some shooting schools—such as H&K instructor course in Virginia and Cooper's out in Arizona—which made me proficient, but I was never completely comfortable teaching it. And there are so many different kinds of weapons in other countries. The first time I ever trained foreign troops with an Uzi, an Israeli 9 mm submachine gun, was the first time that I had ever seen the gun. My team leader assured me that I would be fine—that "in the land of the blind, the one-eyed man is king."

I actually did become fairly good at teaching the basics of shooting—such as stance, body position, grip, sight picture, and trigger squeeze—which apply to every gun that you shoot. I felt like I left the trainees better shots than before they started the class—most of them. We took many from beginner to proficient.

Many of our trainees had never seen a gun when they entered our class. They were understandably afraid of the explosion, or report, and the recoil of the gun in their hands when they shot. I once heard the story of a female Houston police officer that was engaged in a shootout. She fired her gun at a suspect, but dropped the gun and ran the other way, clutching her hand. When other officers finally caught up with her a few blocks away, she was screaming that the gun had "exploded" and injured her hand. They checked her hand—no injuries. They checked her gun—nothing wrong with it. It turned out that she had only shot her gun on the firing range—with ear protection and using a less powerful round of ammunition (.38 versus .357).

Our African trainees had ear protection, but they still didn't like the recoil or report of the weapons. During one session of training, our team leader took a particularly awful group of shooters off the line and confiscated their weapons. He told them that they would probably do better with rocks, and he issued them each a handful. They spent the better part of an afternoon throwing rocks at targets.

Their commanding officers did not take kindly to that kind of humiliation, however, which they thought reflected poorly on them as officers. Later in the day we heard smacking sounds and grunts coming from behind a dirt berm. When we walked to the other side to investigate, we saw an officer beating the students with a bamboo stick. We asked that all future beatings be carried out after class, and they agreed.

We had another particularly poor group of shooters, and no matter how many times we explained sight picture, identifying the dominant eye, or gentle trigger squeeze, the students just could not hit the target, even from close range. We were puzzled until we noticed that they had not removed the gold seal from the lenses of their brand new Ray-Ban sunglasses.

Africans, despite their inexperience with guns, were humble, coachable, and quick to learn. Students in other countries, such as some in Eastern Europe, often had their own way of shooting—taught to them by their Eastern European "comrades"—and were hesitant to follow our instructions. One particularly stubborn major in Romania would not comply with classroom instruction. He preferred to shoot with his body turned sideways, holding the weapon with one hand, arm outstretched, like an Olympic marksman. We attempted several times to explain that this would not work while shooting "combat," and that he could not draw and shoot as quickly or accurately in that position. He would just smile, and every time his turn came to join the line, he would shoot his way. Other students, and his subordinates, began to wonder what they should do—whether they should adapt to this new "Western" style or stick with the major. Mind you, this was immediately after the fall of the Soviet Union, and we were the first western trainers invited to their country.

The conflict eventually reached a head when he challenged our team leader, a fine shot, to a competition. This is often a risky proposition because the trainer is in a no-win situation—if he wins, fine; he should win because he's the trainer. But if he loses, that is not good, and he loses credibility for losing to a student.

Our trainer, Chris, accepted the challenge, probably because he was fed up with this major strutting around, doing it his way, causing a disruption in the class. The two of them loaded their weapons and walked to the line. Chris squared up to the line, shoulders slightly forward, knees slightly bent, right foot six inches back, hands at his belt—the perfect combat stance. Major Know-It-All took his favorite position: sideways.

Let me tell you, the atmosphere was tense. This was not just a battle between two men to decide who shot a sidearm better than the other. This was a battle between East and West, capitalism vs. communism, leather holsters vs. plastic, old school vs. new, my way or the highway. This would decide the fate of the class.

Each was to put two rounds through the target ten meters away. The quickest to do it and still have both rounds pass through center body mass would be the winner. The whistle sounded and both men went for their guns. Both reached at the same time, slapped leather (as John Wayne would say) and began to draw their guns. That's about where the similarities ended.

Chris grabbed his Makarov 9mm in a two-hand grip, raised the gun to eye level, acquired sight picture, and fired a flawless double-tap (two rounds) dead center in the torso on the target. And he did it fast.

The major grabbed for his weapon with his right hand and pulled it from the holster, which had the leather flap folded backward. The next thing we knew, we saw his Makarov slip from his hand and fly up in the air, spinning above his head. We spectators all immediately assumed the stance of someone in fear for his life—one foot slightly back, knees bent slightly, leaning back at the waist, hands in the air. There was an audible gasp from the crowd.

The weapon reached its peak and started to return toward earth, still spinning. The major, who had been waiting for his gun to return, reached out, caught it by the grip, brought it to eye level, and fired. He gave no hint that he had not done it on accident.

The crowd erupted with cheers and applause. We trainers joined in. Slaps on the major's back followed. Nobody had ever seen anything like it. I certainly hadn't. What the major had lost in time was certainly made up in style points. And the competition had ended with best possible outcomes: Chris showed the class that our "capitalist" style of shooting was fast and accurate, and the major was able to save face—kind of. Oh yes, and one other thing—none of us got shot.

I know that my brother Craig and my gun-freak friends will always wonder why I do not love guns as much as they do. To tell you the truth, I don't know why I failed to make that transition in boyhood evolution from rocks to guns. Just like them, I loved rocks, I threw rocks, I collected rocks as a boy, but somewhere along the line I got off track. For now, I will stick with rocks.

31: DIE LIKE A KING

Chad is dry, hot, and desolate, which makes sense since it is located in the exact center of the Sahara desert. N'Djamena, the capital, is situated on the Chari River, which separates it from Nigeria. It's not a regular stop for most tourists.

My CIA colleagues and I were in Chad in the late 1980s, and most of the folks we ran into, both before and after the trip, referred to N'Djamena as "Bullet City." There were so many bullet holes in the buildings that the walls looked like Swiss cheese. The holes have accumulated over the years, over several wars. Chad has had so many civil wars—every so often there is another one between two tribes, usually the one in power and one that wants to be.

I was not that nervous to travel to a place called Bullet City. To be honest I might even like to be from a similar sounding place. It is a macho name. Maybe it wouldn't be so nice to live there at the time it earned that title—but after the dust has settled. I once lived a few miles from a place called Cut and Shoot, Texas. I wanted to move to Cut and Shoot. I still wish that I had been born in Cut and Shoot.

"Where are you from?"

"Down the road a piece, small town called Cut and Shoot," I'd reply.

Seriously, who would mess with you?

Even still, when I tell people I lived in Texas and they ask where, I reply, "A few miles from Cut and Shoot."

B. D. Foley

Despite the utter devastation in N'Djamena, there was a swimming pool at our hotel, the Sofitel. We spent much of the off hours there trying to stay cool, along with numbers of French Foreign Legion troops lounging around drinking. I set a personal record for holding my breath underwater—three minutes.

This record was partly the result of peer pressure. The two men I was traveling with were both overachievers and had plenty of stories. One had lost a leg in Vietnam but still insisted that he could beat anyone in swimming. He eventually made me race him. I beat him. I tried to keep it close but it's hard to lose to a one-legged swimmer unless you are a no-legged swimmer.

The pool attendant was a huge black man with the largest hands I had ever seen. He spoke very little French. One day I asked him, mainly in sign language, where I could go jogging outside the hotel grounds. He did the windshield wiper with one finger (meaning "No, don't do that"), and then the universal sign of a machine gun and rat-a-tat-tat sound. I decided to restrict my exercising to the hotel grounds.

There is a tendency to shoot first and not-even-bother-to-ask-questions later in many countries of Africa. In a neighboring country, one of our US officials decided to drive over to the presidential compound, which was heavily guarded by armed soldiers. Unfortunately, he had neglected to call first and announce his visit. As he drove up to the gate, an armed guard looked at my colleague, who was just sitting there in his vehicle waiting for the gate to open, and blasted thirty rounds from his Uzi into the official's vehicle. Fortunately many in the poorer countries are not able to practice marksmanship. The American was struck only a couple of times in the shoulder and arm. He wisely backed up and raced away as the soldier was loading another 30-round magazine.

I suppose that the guards at presidential palaces have to be on their toes, considering the number of coups that occur. Presidents in Africa are not often rotated by an election. In one country I visited, a country that even bothers to have an election from time to time, the election officials provide either red or green ballots. The president is regularly reelected by 95 percent. We laugh, but if I was living there I do not think I would risk my life by choosing a red ballot. Given that level of corruption, African heads of state either are killed by a political rival or die in office of old age.

One Chadian I met during this stay was a man named Mohammed. He and his fellow tribesmen had been fighting the Libyans on and off for years. My colleagues and I became friends with him during Ramadan, the Islamic month of fasting. As is the custom during Ramadan, Mohammed and his men ate nothing and drank no water despite that heat. They just chewed on sticks to keep their mouths moist. They were used to the Saharan heat. We were not, and after several hours we were forced to go behind our vehicles and drink water.

One day after Mohammed and his men departed, we eventually walked over to the river and gazed out on the green vegetation that lined its banks. We could not help but admire the amazing African desert that stretched before us, as far as the eye could see. It was so vast, so empty, but so peaceful. It wasn't long before one of us, I'm not sure who, thought of the only rational thing that we could do.

It was more instinct that anything—something triggered by the flowing river, the feel of the warm breeze drying our skin, the hot sun on our faces. We stood there on the bank, all three men in a line, facing the river—three grown men, each with two Uzi submachine guns, one in each hand. We all began firing full-auto into the river, screaming at the top of our lungs and laughing. Trigger-happy. Bad boys. And that is where the expression "trigger happy" was born.

Mohammed was about five feet tall and maybe 120 pounds when sopping wet, which he was not. He spoke five languages. He smiled all the time and was as kind as could be. But he was one of the most dangerous men I've ever met—at least to Libyans. A colleague informed me that Mohammed had gotten wind of a group of their enemies visiting a third country. Mohammed and his friends flew there the next day, located the hotel where the targets were residing, sneaked in at night, and killed them all as they slept. I tried to be as polite and friendly with Mohammed as I could possibly be.

As dangerous as Mohammed was, I'm not sure if Mohammed survived and is still alive. His tribe, along with his president, were deposed a year or so later. That might have been the end of Mohammed and his men. It was definitely the end of the expensive armored vehicle that we had provided them. And I'm sure that there are now even more bullet holes in Bullet City.

In addition to being a killer, Mohammed was a philosopher. One brutally hot afternoon, we were talking about different cultures, families, and marriage. He remarked, "A single man lives like a king, but dies like a dog. A married man lives like a dog, but dies like a king." I hope Mohammed has not yet died like a king.

32: PYGMIES AND PYTHONS

The first time I visited Cameroon I crossed the Chari River in a dugout canoe from Chad. The second time I visited, I traveled by a more conventional method, at least for the twenty-first century—an airplane.

A Cameroonian soldier was the one who taught me how to hunt chimpanzees. There is a right and wrong way to do everything, even hunting primates. First, cover your eyes with one hand, the one not holding your spear, in case the chimpanzee throws excrement in an attempt to blind you. You then take your spear, while dodging excrement, and act like you are breaking it across your knee. You do this in case you miss him with the spear and the chimpanzee grabs it and throws it back at you. That is just one more way that you do not want to die—speared by a chimpanzee after it threw crap in your eyes—and have to chase Sgt. Rock about at the campfire in heaven.

If you miss your target, the chimpanzee, which are known to imitate humans, will have seen you attempt to break the spear across your knee, and he will then try to break it. But given his strength, he will succeed in breaking the spear and will not be able to kill you with a broken spear. I don't remember him telling me what to do at that point, after you miss—probably just return home and wash off the crap.

This Cameroonian soldier gave me other advice, such as how to sleep around snakes. According to him, the pygmies of his country are experts in dealing with snakes. Pygmies, he said, are very clever people, and they sleep with their legs apart. He explained that they sleep with their legs apart to avoid being swallowed by a python. You see, if a pygmy is being swallowed at night and has at least one leg free from the snake's mouth, he can stand and fight, or maybe hop to the next hut and ask for help.

I've always heard that snakes often swallow their prey headfirst. So if I were a pygmy, sleeping in an equatorial jungle, I would sleep with my legs apart and my arms sticking out, like a starfish.

My dad never did like snakes. One summer day my brothers and I hiked into the mountains near our town and shot and killed a rattlesnake with our BB guns. I thought it would be funny to roll it up in an old coffee can that I found by the side of the road. My dad soon arrived in our old station wagon to take us home. I waited until he was driving down the road to show him the snake, which I had carefully positioned, coiled up and with the head on top, looking at him. As I lifted the lid on the coffee can, I saw the shock on his face at the sight of a coiled rattlesnake, right under his nose. We laughed as he struggled to stay in the vehicle, while also trying to keep it from careening off the road.

I think that he might have slept like a starfish that night.

33: HUG A TOILET

I'm grateful for toilets. Most of us might not appreciate a toilet, or toilet paper, until we can't find one. I know that many do not appreciate indoor toilets either. My college biology professor once told us about a man who sat down in an outhouse in a mountain campground. Unfortunately, he forgot to first take a stick and swirl it around the opening to get rid of spiders, which is about the best advice I can give a man, and about all I can remember learning during my college years. He was bitten right on his very vulnerable appendage by a black widow spider. So careless, so like Mr. Wheat.

One day, I had to urinate really bad after a basketball game. I had injured my back during the last game of a basketball tournament sponsored by the US embassy in Greece. I was in so much pain that I was unable to even make it to my feet, so the marine security guards laid me on a stretcher and loaded me into their van for the drive home.

As we turned on to Kifisias Avenue, a major thoroughfare of Athens, we were quickly swallowed up in Athens traffic, which is stop and go, stop and go, most of the day. I soon *really, really, really* had to go—my bladder had become much more painful than my lower back injury. I first asked, then pleaded with the marines to pull over somewhere, anywhere—a park or a vacant lot. They reacted like you would expect marines would—they laughed.

But as soon as I threatened to pee in their van, they relented and quickly pulled over to the curb. A marine jumped out of the front passenger seat, slid the side door open and said, "Okay, you want to pee, so pee."

As I lay there, looking at the passing pedestrians on the sidewalk as they looked at me, I wondered briefly if I could relieve myself in front of passersby. Growing up, one of my friends could not pee next to anyone else at a neighboring urinal—I think that the condition is called "bashful bladder." I have never had that problem, until that day in the van.

I decided to go. I rolled over to my side, took aim, and peed out of the open door and into the gutter. And as I relieved myself I closed my eyes in relief, and embarrassment, but also pride. I was certain that I would blow away Scott's urination record from that high school football trip. I kick myself for not timing it.

I learned that day, in that marine van, that sometimes happiness is having a place to pee. I'm grateful for toilets because I've been without so often. There are the overnight camps, of course, with the Boy Scouts, where boys are conditioned to urinate in the wild. Heck, to a boy, the world is a toilet. That's nothing really to brag about, but it's true. Boys can *go* anywhere, even in the bathtub. Can we at least agree that the bathtub should be off-limits?!

My wife and I were watching TV late one night and saw one of our sons walk by. Curious, I followed him into our bedroom, where I saw him peeing into a laundry basket. In his half-asleep state, the basket must have looked a lot like a toilet. My dad, a World War II vet, used to tell us an old joke. Mutt and Jeff are walking along and Mutt has to urinate. A police officer walks by, sees Mutt peeing, and barks at him, "Don't you know that's against the law?" Mutt yells back, "No, it's not. It's against the fence." My dad must have told us that joke during every fishing trip and laughed every time.

I gained an even greater appreciation for toilets while serving in Afghanistan—I was there for the first anniversary of the September 11 attacks. I was assigned to an area south of Kabul. We lived in what I would describe as a mud fort. Many Afghans construct their houses, or compounds—groups of dwellings around a courtyard, surrounded by a large wall—out of their most plentiful building material: dirt. We would often see them building homes while we patrolled. Usually two of them could erect one in short order—one on the ground mixing the mud and tossing it up to the second, who stood on the wall and plopped the mud down, higher and higher. A particularly heavy rain storm actually washed away one of the walls of our fort before I arrived. I didn't find a three-walled compound particularly secure. We joked that all the Taliban needed was a fire truck to wash us out of the valley.

Going "number one" was not a problem. Our camp had "piss tubes" located in the parking area, or courtyard of our mud fort. The piss tubes resembled mortar tubes, sticking up out of the ground at a 45-degree angle. They weren't much, and they smelled bad, but a person got used to it. Our men and women in the military and the CIA, among other agencies, adapt to any hardship that is thrown at them.

For "number two," our toilet was located fifteen feet up a ladder, inside one of the remaining walls. The ladder was a rickety, hand-made, wooden structure made from poles. The rungs were very far apart; going up was a lot easier than climbing down. And doing it in the dark, at night, was even trickier. One of our officers broke his leg climbing down that ladder.

One night at about 3:00 a.m., I struggled to make it up the ladder, weak from a few days of dysentery, and carrying a flashlight and a bucket—for vomiting. A National Guard medic waited for me at the bottom of the ladder. I sat there, fluids leaving my body from whatever exit they could find. I dreaded the thought of going back down the ladder, so I sat there and the thought actually crossed my mind: *If they are ever accurate with the rockets, let it be now.*

The latrine itself was worse than the ladder. The opening was covered by a canvas flap with a little red flag hanging from a string. The flag was to advise others that it was occupied. The latrine never stayed occupied for very long, except for when we had eaten an MRE ("Meals that Refuse to Exit," as we called them).

The latrine consisted of a small mud room and a small mud bench covered by a wooden seat and lid. The mud walls were dry and cracked; practically every one of the hundreds of cracks held burnt incense sticks. And that is the first thing a person had to do upon entering, after holding his breath: light several Indian incense sticks, poke them in the holes in the surrounding walls, and then breathe again, through his mouth, lightly. And that is where my National Guard colleagues also kept their pornography. More incense and pornography, just like in our garage hut all those years prior. Weird.

The sticks helped camouflage the stench of years of excrement at the bottom of the hollow wall, but not completely. I now realize that I could have tried a solution that I came up with back in my days with the Forest Service. A sewer pipe on a government trailer had fallen off, and the occupants did not find out about it for weeks. Dale Goldtooth, a Navajo Indian colleague, and I were tasked with reattaching the pipe. We were on the verge of vomiting just approaching the area; it smelled that bad. Dale liked to chew tobacco, and he offered me some. I felt that if ever I needed it, it was now. I took some from his can and stuffed it up both nostrils. It burned, but it worked. I never smelled a thing. Actually, I didn't smell anything for quite some time after that.

Back to our Afghan bathroom. After finishing in our mud toilet, we had to quickly stand up, grab the lid, throw the paper as quickly as possible down into the hole, and slam the lid shut. If we were not fast enough, the wind, an evil draft that flowed through the hollow walls, would blow the paper right back into our faces.

When I returned from that first trip to Afghanistan, I would sometimes wake up at night to relieve myself. I swung my legs around to the floor and began searching for my boots—which I used to keep under my cot—so I could walk out of our building, down the steps, and across the gravel. I looked and looked before realizing through the fog of drowsiness that I didn't need my boots. I could just walk ten feet across plush carpet onto smooth tiles to a clean porcelain toilet. I didn't have to put on boots, climb a ladder, or light any incense. And I didn't have to swirl a stick around to get rid of spiders.

Now, I do not mean to denigrate the Afghan toilet. They are better than nothing—which is what many people in the rest of the world and Boy Scouts use. In much of the Middle East the bathroom has a hole in the floor and tiles, some with imprinted footprints on each side. Not at all conducive for reading the newspaper.

I worked in Khartoum, Sudan, in the early 1990s. Many Sudanese citizens prefer the outdoor toilet—the ground. Khartoum is located at the fork of the White and Blue Nile rivers. It is a beautiful area if you stay close to the water. The rest of the country is very arid. It is, after all, in the middle of the Sahara. Upon arrival, an officer advised that Sudan is known for having the highest airborne fecal matter content in the world. That is because there are no rest stops with bathrooms for desert travelers. People defecate, it dries up, the wind blows, and there you have it—flying excrement. We were told that respiratory infections among the community were common.

We left our meeting with the urge to hold our breath, but that's hard to do for a month. And I had no chewing tobacco. So we just got used to it. People eventually stop thinking about unpleasant things. But just to give East Coast folks something to think about—much of the dust swirling around eastern homes actually catches a ride on the jet stream and blows in from clear across the Atlantic Ocean, from an area called . . . the Sahara desert. So that is not just dust on your fireplace mantel and grand piano and dishes. That is a special dust from Sudan. How long can you hold your breath?

34: BAD FLIGHTS

One challenge to overseas travel is keeping track of the currency. Every country has its own money, usually with a picture of its current president, if we can call him that. We traveled so much that it was difficult to remember each currency—pounds, francs, dinars, zaires, pesos. We could not remember what each country called its money, and certainly not the exchange rates. So we began referring to all the various currencies by one name—*scoots*. I don't know who made the word up, but it worked. *Do you have any scoots? Lend me a scoot. Let's go to the bank and get some more scoots.*

Another challenge to traveling was the flights. Anyone that has traveled very much has had a bad experience with an airline, most often on a bad flight. I certainly have. I spent one flight from Yaoundé to Douala, Cameroon, in the airplane bathroom with a bad case of diarrhea. There were no flight attendants on board, so no one was there to tell me to find my seat before landing. I couldn't have anyway, even if they had—I was that sick. There's nothing like a case of third-world diarrhea to make you ignore any suggestions that you return to your seat and place your tray in the upright position.

My "flight from Hades" was from Kinshasa, Democratic Republic of the Congo, to Paris, France. The flight had been canceled twice, so there was a backlog of desperate passengers. We all arrived at the airport and wanted seats on the replacement flight, a Middle Eastern Airlines flight. It was all open seating (and open hostilities) among passengers—and various embassy "expeditors"—to find a seat. In hindsight, if we had known how bad the flight was going to be, we would have all been much more polite and ready to let others take our place.

Service was dismal. Soon after takeoff, flight attendants began to make their rounds, slapping unwrapped sandwiches, complete with wilted lettuce, on our tray tables. I noticed that they looked even less thrilled than we were to be on the plane.

I noticed that I was in a fight for legroom—not with another passenger but with a snarling little poodle that belonged to the passenger seated in front of me. The passenger was much more comfortable having his dog under his seat and in my space. I spent much of the next hour slowly pushing the dog forward until I had some room for my feet.

After several hours, we landed in Niamey, Niger, to gas up. If you look at the map, Niger is another country located in the middle of the Sahara. Even though it was hotter than Hades, the airline crew had to shut down the air conditioner to fuel for the entire hour or so that we sat out on the tarmac. The air in the aircraft was stifling and began to smell like a locker room as we all began to sweat.

We finally took off again and were heading across the Mediterranean. About halfway across, however, the plane suddenly began to descend and the pilot's heavily accented voice came over the loudspeaker, "Ladies and gentlemen, we have a cracked cockpit windscreen. We will continue our travels from a lower altitude. Thank you." We descended. The plane just seemed to grow hotter and hotter.

As we began our descent into Paris, we had the feeling that our nightmare flight was over. After eleven or twelve hours on the plane, passengers seemed to be ready to revolt. Many of the passengers were looking out the window, longing for fresh air and some ground beneath their feet. About ten feet off the runway, as the plane was ready to touch down, however, the pilot suddenly hit the gas, pulled up sharply, and then swerved to the left. My colleague and I looked at each other, pressed back into our seats from the surge of speed, wondering if we were going to die or if we were victims of some prank show, waiting for Ashton Kutcher to show up.

Again the pilot's voice: "I am sorry; there was another plane on the runway. We will try again. Thank you." We didn't like the fact that he said he would "try again." We preferred that he just did it, rather than try. And why do people in the service industry insist on saying "thank you" after they have bungled something? Thank you for tolerating our mistakes? Thank you for not rising up and starting a mutiny?

We made another loop around Paris and the pilot "tried again"— this time successfully. As we taxied up to the terminal, passengers began jumping up and retrieving items from the overhead compartment before the plane had come to a complete stop. Everyone wanted off that plane. But just as the plane came to a complete stop, the entire plane shook and lurched sideways, throwing many of the passengers off balance. As we picked ourselves up, we looked out the window and saw that a large catering truck had crashed into the wing, imbedding itself into the back of one of the wings, crushing the flaps.

Back at the office I told that story to a friend, a former Secret Service (USSS). He just smiled and replied, "That's nothing."

According to my friend, his previous colleague had traveled to eastern Africa as part of an advance team to prepare hotel accommodations, transportation, and especially security. During the trip his friend had come down with a serious case of dysentery. He was eventually hospitalized, but his condition was not improving in the very humble local hospital. With no sign that he was recovering, he asked his team to put him on the next plane—to anywhere.

The next flight happened to be to London. He checked his luggage and boarded with nothing but a trench coat. He was so exhausted that he immediately fell deep asleep. Unfortunately, he was so sick and tired that he awoke to find that he had "messed himself." He tried to somewhat clean himself up in the aircraft bathroom. When the plane finally landed in London, the poor secret service agent tried to do the best he could during the short layover, but he did not have much time. He hurried back onto his connection across the Atlantic to Washington, DC. He fell asleep again.

You can guess what happened when he fell asleep again. No, you can't. His body just kept secreting various liquids. When he woke up, the poor man looked around and noticed fellow passengers looking at him, including flight attendants, who asked if he was okay. He had now begun to smell like something unearthly, maybe frightening. He put on his trench coat, wrapped the long tails around his legs, and buttoned it to the top to help cover the smell. It didn't help much. Others in first class began to whisper among themselves, "Who is this man in the trench coat that has sneaked into first class? Is he going to explode?"

We all have bad days. After hearing about this man's experience, I never had another bad flight.

35: GRAY MEETS TANGERINE

In the early 1990s I found myself in Bucharest, Romania. A team of American officers and I were there from late winter through early spring. The Romanians were probably wary of us, one of the first teams of Westerners to visit Bucharest after the fall of President Ceauşescu.

I suppose you'd call it the "fall" of Ceauşescu since he and his wife both fell after the revolutionaries lined them against a wall and machine-gunned them. Romanian officials showed us the video of the execution before we toured the couple's palace and marveled at its opulence and luxurious features, right down to the gold bathroom fixtures.

I suppose that I wouldn't blame the Romanians for being a little wary. They had been taught for decades that capitalists were out to destroy the world. Even now communist dictators continue to spout the same drivel. What they must not know is that the West has never been out to destroy the world. We want to buy their country, maybe, but not destroy it.

Albania was similarly closed off and paranoid during the Cold War. For years Albanian citizens were constantly reminded by their authoritarian government that the United States was about to attack any day. During a visit I made to Albania, I noticed some of the seven hundred thousand bunkers that were constructed around the country, all to prepare for an imminent attack. There was no attack, as we know, and the bunkers served no purpose. After the Cold War ended, a US general encountered a military leader from Albania at a conference. The Albanian officer introduced himself, saying that he was from Albania. The US general replied, "Oh, that's interesting. Could you tell me where your country is located?"

When we arrived in Romania the weather was cold and gray. There were small groups of people waiting in lines outside drab-looking bakeries. I remember pedestrians walking through gray winter streets with gray overcoats. That's the color that I remember—gray coats, gray hats, gray faces. But my most vivid memory of Bucharest is jogging with my friend John.

John was about as nice a guy as one can imagine. He was just genuinely warm. For example, there was a small contingent of North Korean government officials also staying in our hotel. We shared a small breakfast area with representatives from other countries, including the North Koreans. Each country featured their national flag in the middle of the table. They knew who we were, and we knew who they were.

The first couple of mornings the two groups glanced at each other suspiciously. We eyed them; they eyed us. But leave it to John to break the ice. Subsequent mornings, John began bowing and saying, "Good morning," very formally, as we entered and exited. And he said it with a huge smile. Despite his niceness, he never was able to befriend them or get any of them to respond, or smile, other than a few grunts after a week or two.

I think that many warm people, like John, expect others to be warm too. You might call that being naïve. Maybe John was a bit naïve. I would say that being naïve is often an admirable trait because it is often accompanied by genuine friendliness.

Like I said, Romania was cold at that time of year. My hotel room was so cold that I often hopped into the shower to get warm. The water was barely lukewarm, so it didn't help much. The only sure way to get warm was by exercising. John was an avid jogger, and he pressed me daily to run with him. I finally agreed to go for a run, mostly so I wouldn't freeze to death.

B. D. Foley

That afternoon I arrived at the front of the hotel before him. As I waited for John, I warmed up in my old-fashioned gray sweats. I've never been one for fashion, and I have stuck with the old gray sweats since I was a kid. And gray was the fashionable color in Romania of the early 1990s, it seems, so I fit in.

As I warmed up, I noticed a flash of light coming down the steps of the hotel. I looked up and saw John in all his splendor, prancing down the steps in a tight spandex bottom and matching T-shirt. Much of the outfit was pink and purple. My wife would have called it fuchsia and lavender. Women know many more colors than men do. I think that most men have a color vocabulary of about eight—the same number as crayons in the economy box.

I tried not to look at John. Seeing a guy in tights is a little like seeing someone with a booger on their nose—or a guy with his zipper down. You try not to notice. When I was around twenty-one years of age, I was teaching Sunday School in my hometown. The class was made up of a bunch of teenage girls around fifteen to sixteen years old—the worst age. I taught what I thought was an interesting, thought-provoking, well-organized lesson, and felt rewarded when a group of them lingered after the lesson and approached to thank me—or so I thought. The spokesperson stepped forward and said, "Just thought you'd like to know, your zipper was down the entire time." I turned away to zip and then spun back and asked why she hadn't told me earlier. "Why would I do that?" she replied sardonically.

I tried to ignore John as we began our run. I tried to ignore the fact that I was running through the streets of Bucharest with a guy in fuchsia tights. I won't go into any further description here, but his spandex running tights did not leave much to the ladies' imaginations. I hoped and prayed that these gray-coated Romanians would not notice. My hopes were soon dashed.

Cars driving by in the busy boulevard slowed or stopped as they passed us. Pedestrians approaching in our direction stopped in their tracks and watched us. I ran slower, hoping that John would leave me behind, but John would just slow down too. I decided that my only chance was to get off the city streets and away from traffic, so I suggested a park.

The park wasn't any better. Families who were strolling along through the lanes of trees stopped in their tracks. Children gawked and pointed as their parents reached down to cover their eyes. I now realized that there was no escape. I had to return to the safety of the hotel, and quickly.

As we turned at the end of the park to head back toward the hotel, I began to increase my speed. I have never run so fast for so long. I raced past more gawking Romanians who had set out for a stroll, not knowing that it would include a show. I do not know what they thought, frankly.

We made it back to the hotel in no time. John commented on how much he enjoyed the run and the brisk pace. I decided that I had to be honest. I confessed that I had run so fast for one reason, and that was because I didn't enjoy running with men in pink tights. John looked down at his spandex as if he was surprised, but he admitted grudgingly, "Yeah, I guess my running outfit did attract a little attention. But they're not pink, they're fuchsia."

"A little attention? A *little* attention?" I repeated. "I'll tell you what," I added, "I'm not going running with you ever again unless you find something else to wear. I'm not going through that again." John agreed to wear something else.

The next day, John suggested that we go jogging, without his spandex. I was waiting in front of the hotel again, stretching, warming up in my gray sweats under the gray skies, with people in gray overcoats walking by, when out popped John, again arrayed in all of his splendor—a pair of tiny silk jogging shorts. These were running shorts, the kind with slits going all the way up the side, to the waistband. They were not fuchsia but some other fluorescent color not found in my color vocabulary of eight words. Frankly, when I dared look at him, I quickly realized that those shorts would cover a little more in the front than his spandex had, but less in the back. I pictured more Romanian women gawking, men laughing, children crying, cars crashing.

I looked down at my feet, and my gray sweats, wondering what to tell John.

"John," I began carefully, "when I told you to wear something else, I didn't mean this new outfit. Don't you have a pair of sweats, maybe something in gray?"

"No," replied John.

"Well, then, have a good run."

I sprinted past John and up the stairs to the hotel entrance, back to the cold but safe hotel. John went ahead with his running and introduced Bucharest to orange—or rather, tangerine.

36: LOYALTY

I do not have good feelings about my grandpa, though I never met him. I told you I'm bad. I'm bad enough to hate my own grandpa.

My dad was just a baby when my grandpa, David Arthur, and his brother Joe, went off to Europe to fight the Germans. World War I had been raging, and American men like my grandpa and uncle threw in to help end the war that H. G. Wells referred to as "the war to end war." Yep, he missed that one by a few wars. A few months into the war, Uncle Joe was struck by a mortar and killed instantly. His fellow soldiers hastily buried him in a temporary grave, and he was forgotten like thousands of others.

My grandpa David did not forget, however, and even after the war ended, he stayed on in France to search for Joe's body. He eventually joined the US Military Graves Commission to help in the effort. He found Joe's body, but unfortunately, Grandpa David also found a new wife—Germaine, a French woman.

I do not know what he was thinking. He had a wife and four boys back in Massachusetts waiting for him to return, writing letters, worrying, trying to survive. Was Grandpa David worrying about them, writing letters, right until he met Germaine? Was he overcome with grief after the loss of his brother Joe? I don't know. Maybe I won't judge him too harshly, because war is hell. But I do know that he was not loyal to his wife and children back in America.

Should I tell other stories about men who were not loyal? Should I tell you the story of a colleague who was shot and killed when he was out with prostitutes? Should I tell you stories of other colleagues who were unfaithful to their wives or girlfriends during travel overseas? Would it help if I provided statistics on how many marriages have been ruined and torn apart, on how many families have been destroyed because of a lack of loyalty? Would it?

One day, in the CIA, I was speaking to a colleague about security clearances and the administration of polygraph (or lie-detector, as some call it) examinations that we had to undergo every so many years. It was not pleasant, I'll admit. The polygraph exam is about as pleasant as a colonoscopy, only the "patient" is awake during the procedure. And polygraph examiners are not chosen because they are pleasant. They sit across from the examinee and do their best to make him feel uncomfortable. It doesn't take much, either, being hooked up to wires, the wires to a machine, subjected to uncomfortable questions tailored to make one feel uncomfortable, all to find out if the subject is . . . loyal. Thousands of dollars, millions of dollars, actually, to find out if the applicant, or employee, is loyal.

It would seem, therefore, that the government, and especially the CIA, must be very concerned to know if a person is loyal.

But during my conversation with my colleague, I was silly enough to bring up the concept that not only should we be loyal to the government, to the CIA, and to our Constitution, but we should also be loyal to our spouse.

"What?" he asked.

"I think that an operations officer should also be loyal to his wife, and those questions should be part of the polygraph exam," I replied.

A look of puzzlement seemed to spread across his face.

"Well, that's probably overdoing it, don't you think? They couldn't ask that," he said.

"No, I don't think it's overdoing it. Loyalty is loyalty. If a man would cheat on his wife or family, don't you think that he would be inclined to cheat on his country?" I reasoned.

He had obviously never followed that line of thinking but decided to find a compromise.

"Well, I don't think it's the same thing. But I agree that it's wrong to let an affair destroy your family, that's for sure."

"I'm glad that you agree," I proffered.

"Well, I'm not talking about 'getting a little on the side.' But, you know, a guy just has to be discreet and not let the affair affect his marriage."

So you see? Disloyalty, or cheating, is fine if he is not caught. Be discreet in your disloyalty, is what he was saying.

I had never heard anyone state it so bluntly, but his outlook was common. In all my years working for the CIA, I was never asked if I was loyal to my wife. During all of my polygraph examinations, a polygrapher never asked if I frequented prostitutes, if I had a mistress, or if I was loyal to my wife or to my family. Maybe the CIA and US government are not that worried about loyalty after all.

Disloyalty comes in many shapes, degrees, and shades, like anything else. Some are not loyal to their favorite sports team, when the team is losing, of course. Some are not loyal to a boss or employer when they bad-mouth the company's product or service to others. I admit there were times that I was not loyal to a girlfriend in college before my marriage. I regret that.

Some commit "virtual infidelity." A friend's daughter was dating a man and they were soon to be engaged. Before the engagement, however, she learned that her boyfriend was an avid porn consumer, probably an addict. She found out that he was disloyal to her digitally. Yes, he was being disloyal to her in his mind. He explained to her that since he had not acted upon his thoughts, that it must be all right. Interestingly, he attempted to convince her that the marriage should proceed, arguing, "Look, you prayed that I was the one for you and you had confirmation from God. And God knows that I watch porn, and he still answered your prayer that you should marry me . . . so God must be okay with it." Do you follow his reasoning? It is not that dissimilar from my CIA colleague's rationalization. "It's okay, as long as it is kept hidden, and no one finds out about it." Do you follow that?

Maybe the porn addict is only cheating in his thoughts, so far, but a cheat is a cheat. Maybe he just hasn't had a chance to carry it out yet. But my friend's daughter figured it out. She dropped him like a hot potato and then stuck a fork in him. He was done.

I believe that God, if there is a God—and I sure hope there is or I'm going to be ticked off when I die and realize that I'm nowhere—would not be okay with him watching smut while he prepares to marry a beautiful young woman whom he does not deserve. God is not okay with it. If you hear otherwise from God, let me know. Otherwise, stop watching pornography.

Be loyal. Be loyal to your country. Be loyal to your girlfriend. Be loyal to your wife. And yes, be loyal to your sports team, especially when they are losing. Go Cowboys!

37: NORMANS REMEMBER

Americans love to hate the French; *snooty, arrogant, ungrateful* are just a few of the adjectives that are tossed at them. Some are arrogant; some are ungrateful—or maybe forgetful—for the American lives lost during the wars. But what many Americans do not understand is that there are many different types of French men and women and more than one France, just as there is more than one America.

Now don't get me wrong. I'm not defending all of the French. But imagine a Frenchman visiting New York City and lumping the more reserved New Yorkers (how's that for political correctness?) in with the neighborly folks from Somerville, Tennessee, or comparing the Harvard crowd of Boston to the people in Cut and Shoot, Texas? While Bostonians might judge the caliber of man by what Ivy League university he attended, Cut and Shoot citizens probably judge a man by the caliber of his gun—and how well he shoots his guns—or the size of his truck. Okay, that might be a slight exaggeration. But even though we are all "Americans," each region of the country has widely divergent political, religious, or cultural identities. And my town probably has much in common with many small towns in the rest of the world, such as Bayeux, France.

You don't hear much from Parisians about the sacrifices of US soldiers during the World Wars, especially not World War I. Maybe they're just not used to saying "thank you" very much, and World War I and World War II happened a long time ago. But not that long ago I helped a man change his tire on Place de La Concorde in my nice suit on my way home from work, and he didn't so much as sniff or say thanks when I finished up, with my fingers all black and greasy. I didn't expect him to express his undying gratitude. And I didn't expect every Frenchman I encountered there to grab me and thank America for her sacrifices. But an occasional "thanks, we appreciate it" would have been nice.

Maybe Parisians are too busy, or maybe they are just in a bad mood. But in Normandy, which is along the northern coast of France, I encountered two elderly women from the small town of Bayeux who still remember.

One beautiful summer day, June 6 to be exact (D-day), my wife and I decided to take our family to Normandy to the landing beaches. We had visited Paris, France several times over the years and knew that we had to take the children there. My father and mother both followed my Uncle Joe and Grandpa David to France, both of them serving in the air force during the Berlin airlift after World War II. And now here I was in France with my family. We could not leave France without visiting Normandy.

We reached the coast after a few hours driving in our 1975 Mercedes-Benz. We had lost (or should I say destroyed) our Mazda in a traffic accident during a previous tour. The Mercedes-Benz was built like a tank, with actual bumpers with shock absorbers built into the front and rear bumpers like battering rams. I often found myself wishing that a French driver in a Smart car would decide to do battle with me. Alas, no such luck. They usually gave me a wide berth, however, suspecting that someone driving a twenty-five-year-old car with bumpers on steroids and rusty holes in the fenders had no fear of an accident. They were correct.

The big problem with that Mercedes, however, was that the air conditioner was out and the heater was always on—all the time. We could just not turn it off, and we were forced to leave the windows open and drive very fast. Short commutes around town were not a significant problem since we could usually arrive at our destination before succumbing to heat exhaustion. The three or so hours to Omaha Beach in the summer, however, would be torturous. Thank heavens we had our newborn, Shana, and her Huggies. The diapers fit nicely into the dash vents and worked well to at least partially block the hot air blasting us in the face. We arrived with red faces, but we were conscious.

We first visited the American cemetery at Omaha Beach, where thousands of our troops were buried after they died storming the beach on D-day and in ensuing battles. The cemetery is meticulously cared for and is a sacred place. Walking among the crosses and stars of David inspires one with a quiet reverence.

We then traveled west along the coast to Pointe du Hoc. Pointe du Hoc is located between Utah Beach to the west and Omaha Beach to the east. During World War II the Germans had constructed massive concrete bunkers along the coast as part of the Atlantic Wall. The 155 mm guns in the bunkers, which had been captured from the allies and fortified, were a grave threat on both of the landing beaches. Allied forces considered Pointe du Hoc a high value target.

The initial Allied bombing from the air in the days leading up to D-day failed to destroy the bunkers, let alone the guns. The 2nd Ranger Battalion was called upon to assault German forces at Pointe du Hoc and destroy the German guns on December 6, 1944. The assault was the stuff of legends. The Rangers scaled 100-foot cliffs from the small beach area, eliminated the German forces, and destroyed the guns. Their assault on Pointe du Hoc was a success.

Many of the craters from the bombing are still there, covered in green grass, as are the bunkers. My oldest son, Nolan, who was five at the time, began to roll and play in the craters, not understanding the sacrifices made by our troops and not recognizing the sacred nature of the area. I called him to me and took him inside the bunkers to read the plaques and view the ocean from the German point of view.

As we walked into one bunker and began reading a plaque on the wall, two elderly women approached and spoke to me in French.

"*Parlez-vous français?*" one asked.

"*Mais oui,*" I replied, and our conversation continued in French.

"Are you American?"

"Yes, I am."

"We just wanted to say thank you," replied one of the ladies.

I was a little in shock. These two lovely ladies, looking to be in their early seventies, had felt compelled to thank a couple of random

American tourists for something that had occurred more than fifty years earlier. While I recovered, they explained that they were residents of Bayeux—the first city on the coast to be liberated during the D-day assault. They were teenage girls back in 1944, at the time of the assault. After liberation they had remained in Bayeux, raised families, and enjoyed the freedom that American and other Allied troops brought to the continent. On that morning they were just walking along the beach enjoying a stroll and wanted to thank someone. I was grateful that they chose us.

I told them both that my father had served in World War II as a pilot. I added that he had fought in China and had flown in the Berlin Airlift after the war. I promised to pass the thanks on to him. I kept that promise, and told my dad the story several times before he passed away.

I would like to pass the thanks of these two women on to our American soldiers, especially to our World Ward II veterans, most of whom are gone. Most of the world has forgotten the good you have done in the world and remember only the blemishes of fighting a war. Most do not remember the American blood that has been shed to liberate nations from tyranny. But some remember, like these two ladies from Bayeux. They still say thank you. And we all should too. Let's say "thank you" to our veterans.

And while we are at it, let's express appreciation to others who make our lives better, who make our lives worth living. Let's say thanks to our parents, teachers, custodians, doctors, dentists, hotel maids, waiters, cashiers, carpenters, truck drivers. Did I forget anyone? Tell them all thanks. But especially say thanks to our veterans.

38: DAD

My dad's story really began when his father and uncle both enlisted in the army to fight the Germans in January 1918. While the two brothers were trying to survive the gas and horrendous battles of the trenches, my grandfather's wife, Florence, was struggling to survive as well, raising four little boys on her own. The grandparents helped as best as they could, but it was not easy.

When David did not return home after the war, Florence and her children were forced to fend for themselves. They moved back and forth between Watertown, Massachusetts, and the Midwest, sometimes leaving some of the boys with grandparents out of necessity.

As they grew up, the boys didn't have much, so they took odd jobs to help out. Dad worked for a Greek shoe cobbler repairing and shining shoes from the seventh to ninth grades. The grinder he used to polish shoes spit dust in his face for hours at a time, and as a result he developed a spot on his lung as he grew up. He later worked in a pool hall, often throwing dice with customers at the cash register, daring them "double or nothing" over their bill. A regular client of the bar, a man with a glass eye, often dropped it in other patrons' soup accidentally and would then finish the meal when the repulsed owner could not bring himself to eat it.

Florence eventually married another man, an Irishman named John Foley who worked on the Wabash Railroad. This was a great job in the 1920s and '30s, especially after the Great Depression struck the country and made jobs scarce. It was a steady wage. Foley adopted the four boys—no small feat and especially admirable for a man to do during hard times. It seemed that the family's luck had returned.

Ah, the luck of the Irish. Only problem, Foley had a drinking problem. His Wabash bosses soon tired of it, and Foley was fired. Without a job, he decided that it was better to leave than face his wife and the four boys. He followed in David's footsteps and did not return home. Florence and her sons had now been abandoned twice.

Despite their difficulties, my dad never complained much about his childhood. He and his brothers all had enough food and shoes and clothes—but not much else. He got used to simple pleasures; he was accustomed to having enough, and that was good enough. His favorite meal was stuffed peppers, which is nothing more than hamburger stuffing in a pepper. My mom learned how to make it once they married to make him happy. The first time she prepared it she watched with anticipation as he ate the hamburger stuffing, but left the peppers. When she exclaimed, in surprise, that his mother had told her it was his favorite dish, he replied, "Sure I like stuffed peppers. I just don't like the peppers."

Dad enjoyed sports a great deal. A grade school coach once took him to watch a college football game, which inspired my dad to try football and many sports. It's funny how history repeats itself. Fifty years later, Dad took his fifth grade students to see a University of Utah football game. One of the boys, Tommy Westover (how do I still remember that name but can't remember what my wife sends me to get at the grocery store?), disappeared during the game. After searching for half the game, Dad found the boy selling peanuts, wearing a red and white striped uniform. I wonder if Westover's dad had abandoned him too.

Dad played basketball and football and ran track. He set the Missouri state record in the long jump. He worked for the telephone company during the summers, digging holes for telephone poles and stringing wire. All that digging and climbing toughened him up physically. They played football with leather helmets and no face masks. His cheeks and chin were often covered with cuts from kicks in the face during tackles. He got so much grit, some between his teeth, I imagine, that he hurt defenders who tried to tackle him alone.

I always found him to be tougher than nails. One evening during a fishing trip, while my dad was changing a hook, my little brother ran through his fishing line. The treble hook sunk deep into the palm of Dad's hand. My siblings and I were shocked at the injury and stared at his hand in horror. My dad simply took hold of the shank and pushed the point the rest of the way through the flesh of his hand. When it came out the other side, he clipped off the barb with a pair of pliers and pulled it out. We were amazed that he didn't cry. He did it all without much complaint, except to tell us to stay away from his line next time.

After high school, Dad traveled to Southwestern University (now called Rhodes College) in Memphis, Tennessee, to play football. That's where he met Will Rhea Winfrey, a Southern boy who became his lifelong friend. Mr. Will Rhea, as we always referred to him, told me that Dad was a good pass receiver and punt returner. He chuckled that Dad could also get mean when he was drunk and would sometimes pick fights. I guess I can understand some of the pent-up anger he might have had. One night the two friends happened upon a husband who was physically abusing his wife out in the street. My dad stepped in and beat the husband. He regretted it later, having shamed the man in front of his wife.

When they were grown up, Dad's brothers—Ralph, Howard, and Harold—decided that they would change their last name back to Thompson. Dad resisted and asked them why they wanted to change back. He figured that a name is a name. He was the only one of the four brothers who kept the Foley name. "It doesn't really matter what our last name is, since neither of them were any damn good," he reasoned.

He's right. A name is a name, unless it's one of those last names that some are cursed with, like the name of a body part or some other embarrassing meaning. I've been teased all my life about my middle name, Durwood. My friends—once they found out about it—thought it was the funniest name they'd ever heard. Even I used to think that it sounded kind of silly and did not like revealing it when someone asked for my middle name, or when it was required on application forms. It was usually just this "D" stuck there in the middle of my name, like a wart. It wasn't until my dad told me that I was named after a good friend, Durwood Harper, a fellow pilot who died in China during World Ward II, that I warmed up to the name. I sometimes even volunteer it before I am asked.

We didn't know a lot about my dad's years in World War II until we read about him in *Wing to Wing*, by Carl Molesworth, a book about my dad's outfit, the Chinese-American Composite Wing, which operated in China during the war. I've heard that this is normal humility for many World War II veterans—they do not boast about their service. I mean seriously, who else would refer to the Himalayas, or Mount Everest, as "the hump" but a bunch of pilots who crossed them in unsophisticated, unpressurized bombers?

My dad decided to enlist after college, and he hitchhiked from Tennessee to Alabama to join the Army Air Corps. He passed the test to become a pilot and began to fly bombers. The year was 1940, and his first assignment was to Langley Air Force Base in Virginia. During the next couple of years, he learned to fly B-25s, B-26s, and trainers. He was assigned to Tampa Bay as an instructor pilot and trained new pilots on the B-26, which Dad described as a worthless plane. He said that they had the saying, "One a day in Tampa Bay," which referred to the number of planes that crashed in the water.

In 1943 Dad was called up to fight in China. He joined the Fourteenth Air Force and traveled from Florida across the Atlantic, stopping along the way in Libya, Iran, and finally Pakistan, at the foot of the Himalayas. He commanded the first bomber squadron in a combat mission over that "hump" on October 25, 1943, the first high-altitude mission for the Chinese-American Combat Wing (CACW). He never told us this, but reading in *Wing to Wing*, we learned that Dad was the top bombardment pilot in the CACW, credited with having sunk 28,000 tons of Japanese shipping.

Upon his arrival in Kunming, China, Dad was summoned by the officer-of-the-day to meet with General Chenault, a legend in the Fourteenth Air Force. He was nervous to meet General Chenault, a French Cajun, but learned that the general was a kind man who was nevertheless a master tactician. He had previously organized and run the famous Flying Tigers and would now command the Fourteenth

Air Force. During their meeting, General Chenault advised that he had just met with President Roosevelt, who had assigned him the mission of destroying Japanese shipping.

Much of the bombing was accomplished with "skip" bombs. Pilots would swoop in low toward their target and release their bombs fifty feet off the water. The bombs would skip toward the ship, then sink below the water line and detonate underwater, rupturing the hull at its most vulnerable point and sinking the ship.

One of the few stories we managed to drag from Dad was about his being shot down while attacking Japanese shipping at Amoy Harbor in China. Both his and a member of his squadron's planes were struck by heavy anti-aircraft fire. He described the flashes of guns far below as "blinking" at his aircraft. The other bomber began to fall behind during the return to base. Despite damage to his own plane— his engine was already running roughly—Dad circled back to check on the other pilot, inspecting the aircraft from the outside to assess the damage. As he did, he lost an engine and soon realized that he would never make it over the 6,000-foot mountains along the coast. He ordered his crew to bail out before he also jumped as the plane was going down. Interestingly, his aircraft had Chinese and American markings on the fuselage, for just such an occasion.

The crew was spread out over several miles of Chinese farmland. Dad landed in a grove of trees but was uninjured. He soon heard people searching for them and hoped that they were Chinese and not Japanese troops. When he eventually dared look out from behind a cluster of trees, he saw a Chinese woman looking at him, peering from behind another tree. They both froze and quickly ducked back into hiding. A minute later, they both looked again, and then retreated behind their trees. The third time Dad looked, he spotted the lady running up a trail toward the village.

The villagers eventually managed to gather the entire crew from the countryside and escorted them to their village. Farmers soon advised them that the Japanese were looking for the American crew, and the crew and villagers quickly set out in the opposite direction. Several villagers carried one of his injured crew in a "sedan chair" and went at such a furious clip that he had a hard time keeping up. As they traveled and passed through neighboring villages, children threw firecrackers, which they believed would ward off evil spirits. The explosions made the crew very nervous, as it sounded like gunfire; Dad had to stop himself from reaching for his sidearm.

The group eventually reached the residence of the chief of the Guangdong province, who decided to make "political hay" by organizing parties and feasts at various villages in the area. At one gathering, Dad and the crew were eating at a well-to-do Chinese home. One of his crew went out on a balcony to stretch his legs and noticed a crowd of people had gathered to see the American airmen. He raised his arms and the crowd cheered. When he would lower his arms, the crowd would stop. Arms up, cheers, arms down, silence, up—cheers, down—silence. After a half-dozen times or so, Dad yelled at the aspiring orchestra conductor to knock it off.

The crew was eventually transferred to trucks, where they made it farther inland to Sichuan, then a train to Hengyang. They finally caught a flight back to their air base at Guilin. He and his crew had survived.

My dad did not hold that much of a grudge against the Japanese but never could bring himself to purchase a Japanese appliance or car for the remainder of his life. He did not seem angry. He just wanted to "buy American."

After World War II Dad flew in the Berlin Airlift, where he met my mother, who was working for the air force in Wiesbaden. He then flew in the Korean War and later in the Strategic Air Command, where he and his fellow pilots flew "nukes" around the clock. In all, he served in the air force for twenty years—which included two wars, and three if you include the Cold War. Not bad for a poor twice-abandoned boy from Missouri.

Interestingly, they call Missouri the "Show Me" state. I'd say that he showed us.

A few years before he died, my dad went to visit his old teammate, Will Rhea, who had lost his eyesight. He brought another old friend, who had only one eye left. Will Rhea took them to tour a Civil War battlefield in Shiloh, which is not far from Will Rhea's home in Somerville, Tennessee. The three old friends eventually became lost in the battlefield, driving around in circles. My dad, still the pilot, complained, "Well, I'm in a hell of a mess. I have a one-eyed copilot and a blind navigator."

39: THE BLIND NAVIGATOR

Many people comment that Dad and the other running backs of Southwestern University looked like the Four Horsemen. Some tough-looking guys—short hair, chiseled features, strong frames. My dad is on the left. The player next to him is his old friend, that blind navigator, Will Rhea Winfrey. I got to know Will Rhea after my dad's death in 2005. I have to tell you about Will Rhea.

Will Rhea was from Somerville, Tennessee. He cleared the county road along the family property with a team of horses. He told me that when he was only seven years old, he moved from their family home, which was a hundred and fifty or so years old, into an adjoining structure, a small farm tackle room, where they kept farm implements and horse tack and supplies. He had a small wood stove to keep warm during the winters. Will Rhea was made of stout stuff. He had grit.

Will Rhea joined the army about the same time that my dad joined the Army Air Corps, which became the air force. He served in the European theatre during World War II. When he returned he continued an army career but suffered a degenerative eye disease. He married and had children but eventually became completely blind.

When my dad died I wanted to stay in touch with Will Rhea. In a way, Will Rhea was a connection to the past, to my dad. I would call him from time to time, even when I was overseas. While in Iraq I tried to call him several times over a month or so and could not reach him. Worried, I kept trying every day and finally found him home after quite some time. When he finally answered, I asked him where he had been. He told me that his wife had been driving their vehicle and had suffered a heart attack and died. The only thing he knew was that he found himself in a ditch, with his wife next to him. When they were rescued from the vehicle, the EMTs were unable to save his wife. Will Rhea had suffered broken ribs and had recovered in the hospital.

I was amazed at his attitude. Over the next few years, I kept in touch and would often call him. On a Friday night he would routinely tell me when he answered, in his wonderful, Southern drawl, "Well, I'm sitting he-ah with my relatives, having my Friday night 'communion.' Now, you're a Mormon, so you must not be familiar with Friday night communion." He would chuckle each time.

When I retired from the CIA I decided to stop in and visit him on our way back to Utah. We drove through Somerville to see him. During one of our conversations, I asked him how he managed to stay so upbeat despite the challenges he had faced in his life, being ninety years old, blind, and living alone since losing his wife. He smiled and commented softly, "Well, any morning I can wake up and put my two feet on the floor, it's a good day."

That's it, to be grateful. It is about the best advice I can give a man, other than to make sure to swirl a stick around an outhouse toilet before sitting down. Be grateful that you can see, because some can't. Be grateful that you can put your two feet on the floor, because some, like a friend with whom I served in Afghanistan, no longer can. Appreciate your parents. Appreciate your family, friends, and wife. Appreciate the people in your life.

Okay, that was definitely my last rhyme.

Get out of here. Put your feet on the floor. Now get up.

ABOUT THE AUTHOR

B. D. FOLEY is a retired covert operations officer with the Central
Intelligence Agency (CIA). His career led him to far-flung places,
adventure, friendship, and even a wife he "recruited" in the Congo. As
an intelligence officer in the world of espionage, he hunted for sources
and was hunted by others in turn. Since retirement he has mostly
avoided hunting of any kind but kept busy building a barn, raising
children and chickens, working as a job coach for the disabled, and
teaching classes as a substitute teacher—the latter pursuit being probably his most challenging endeavor! The Foley family resides in Utah.

SCAN TO VISIT

0   26575 19202   5

WWW.BDFOLEY.COM